A

# TREATISE

ON THE

# MILLENNIUM

BY SAMUEL HOPKINS, D. D.

## ARNO PRESS

A NEW YORK TIMES COMPANY

New York • 1972

Reprint Edition 1972 by Arno Press Inc.

Reprinted from a copy in
The Wesleyan University Library

RELIGION IN AMERICA - Series II
ISBN for complete set:  0-405-04050-4
See last pages of this volume for titles.

Manufactured in the United States of America

Publisher's Note:  This volume was reprinted
from the best available copy.

———————◆—●◗●—◆————————

Library of Congress Cataloging in Publication Data

Hopkins, Samuel, 1721-1803.
    A treatise on the millennium.

    (Religion in America, series II)
    Reprint of the 1793 ed., which was issued in the
author's The system of doctrines contained in divine
revelation explained and defended.
    1.  Millennium.  I.  Title.
BT890.H65  1972        236'.3        70-38450
ISBN 0-405-04070-9

A

# TREATISE

ON THE

# MILLENNIUM.

SHOWING from SCRIPTURE PROPHECY,

THAT IT IS YET TO COME;
WHEN IT WILL COME;
IN WHAT IT WILL CONSIST;

AND THE

EVENTS WHICH ARE FIRST TO TAKE PLACE,
INTRODUCTORY TO IT.

⸺⸺

BY SAMUEL HOPKINS, D. D.

Paſtor of the Firſt Congregational Church in NEWPORT, *Rhode Iſland.*

⸺⸺

THIS ſhall be written for the generation to come : And the people, which ſhall
be created, ſhall praiſe the LORD.⸺PSALM CII. 18.

PRINTED AT *BOSTON,*
BY ISAIAH THOMAS AND EBENEZER T. ANDREWS,
PROPRIETORS of the WORK,
FAUST'S STATUE, No. 45, NEWBURY STREET.
MDCCXCIII.

# DEDICATION.

*To the* PEOPLE *who fhall live in the* DAYS *of the*
MILLENNIUM.

HAIL, YE HAPPY PEOPLE, HIGHLY FAVOURED OF THE LORD!

To you the following treatife on the Millennium is dedicated, as you will live in that happy era, and enjoy the good of it in a much higher degree, than it can be now enjoyed in the profpect of it. And that you may know, if this book fhall be conveyed down to your time, what is now thought of you, and of the happy day, in which you will come on the ftage of life. You will be able to fee the miftakes which are now made on this head; and how far what is advanced here, is agreeable to that which is noted in the fcripture of truth, and a true and proper defcription of the events which are to take place; and to rectify every miftake. All is therefore humbly fubmitted to your better judgment.

When you fhall learn what a variety of errors, in doctrine and practice, have been, and are now imbibed and propagated; and in what an imperfect and defective manner they are oppofed and confuted; and the truth explained and defended: And obferve how many defects and miftakes there are in thofe writings which contain moft truth, and come neareft to the ftandard of all religious truth, the holy fcripture, you will be ready to wonder how all this could be, where divine revelation is enjoyed. But your benevolence and candour, will make all proper allowances, for all the

prejudices

prejudices and darknefs which take place in thefe days, and pity us; while your piety will lead you to afcribe the greater light and advantages which you will enjoy, and your better difcerning and judgment, not unto yourfelves, but to the diftinguifhing, fovereign grace of God.

Though you have yet no exiftence, neverthelefs, the faith of the chriftians in this and in former ages, beholds you "at hand to come;" and realizing your future exiftence and character, you are greatly efteemed and loved; and the pious have great joy in you, while they are conftantly, and with great earneftnefs praying for you. They who make mention of the Lord, will not keep filence, nor give him any reft, till he eftablifh, and till he make Jerufalem a praife in the earth. For you they are praying and labouring, and to you they are miniftring; and without you they cannot be made perfect. And you will enter into their labours, and reap the happy fruit of their prayers, toils and fufferings.

They will be in heaven, with the holy angels and the fpririts of the juft made perfect, when you will come upon the ftage in this world; and they will rejoice in you, in your knowledge, benevolence, piety, righteoufnefs and happinefs: And all their paft prayers for you will be turned into joy and praife. And you will, in due time, be gathered together with them unto the Lord Jefus Chrift, in his eternal kingdom, and join in feeing and praifing him forever, afcribing bleffing, and honour, and glory, and power, unto the only true God, the Father, Son, and Holy Ghoft. Amen.

A TREATISE

A

# T R E A T I S E

ON THE

# M I L L E N N I U M.

## *INTRODUCTION.*

A PARTICULAR hiſtory of the church of Chriſt, from the days of the Apoſtles, to this time ; of the various changes through which it has paſt ; of the doctrines which have been taught and maintained ; of the diſcipline, worſhip, and manners, which have taken place ; of the grand apoſtacy in the church of Rome, and of the reformation, &c. might be properly ſubjoined to the foregoing ſyſtem, were it not that this has been done by a number of writers already ; ſo that all who are diſpoſed to acquaint themſelves with eccleſiaſtical hiſtory, may obtain this information by books already extant : Which, at the ſame time, ſerve to confirm the truth and divine original of chriſtianity, by diſcovering, in how many inſtances the ſtate of the church, and the events which have had a particular reſpect to it, have been foretold, and have taken place according to the predictions. This ſubject has been particularly illuſtrated by Mr. Lowman, in his " Paraphraſe and Notes on the Revelation of St. John." And ſince, more largely, by Biſhop Newton, in his " Diſſertation on the Prophecies, which have remarkably been fulfilled, and at this time are fulfilling in the world."

A treatiſe on the Millennium, however, and of the future ſtate of the church of Chriſt, from this time to the end of the world, as it is predicted and deſcribed in divine revelation, is thought

proper

proper and important, not only as it has been more than once re-
ferred to in the preceding work ; but as it appears not to be
believed by many ; and not to be well underſtood by more ; or
attended to by moſt, as an important event ; full of inſtruction ;
ſuited to ſupport, comfort and encourage chriſtians, in the preſent
dark appearance of things, reſpecting the intereſt of Chriſt, and
his church ; and to animate them to faith, patience and perſever-
ance in obedience to Chriſt ; putting on the hope of ſalvation
for an helmet.  And to excite them more earneſtly to pray for
the advancement and coming of the kingdom of Chriſt :  Of
which kingdom, as it is to take place in this world, or of chriſtianity itſelf, there cannot be ſo clear, full and pleaſing an idea,
if the ſcripture doctrine of the Millennium be kept out of view.

In the firſt three centuries after the Apoſtles, the doctrine of
the Millennium was believed and taught ; but ſo many unworthy and abſurd things were by ſome advanced concerning it, that
it afterwards fell into diſcredit, and was oppoſed, or paſſed over
in ſilence, by moſt, until the reformation from popery.  And
then a number of enthuſiaſts advanced ſo many unſcriptural and
ridiculous notions concerning it, and made ſuch a bad improvement of it, that many, if not moſt of the orthodox, in oppoſing
them, were led to diſbelieve and oppoſe the doctrine in general ,
or to ſay little or nothing in favour of the doctrine, in any ſenſe
or view of it.

But few of the moſt noted writers of the laſt century in Britain,
or in other parts of the proteſtant world, have ſaid any thing to
eſtabliſh or explain this doctrine :  And they who have mentioned
it, do appear, at leaſt the moſt of them, not to have well underſtood it.  In the preſent century, there has been more attention
to it ; and the ſcriptures which relate to it, have been more care-
fully conſidered, and explained by a number of writers ; and it
has been ſet in a more rational, ſcriptural and important light,
than before.  Dr. Whitby, has written a treatiſe on the Millennium.  And Mr. Robertſon, and Mr. Lowman, have aſſerted
and explained it in ſome meaſure, in their expoſition of the book
of the revelation by the Apoſtle John ; eſpecially the beginning of
the twentieth chapter of that book.  And the late Preſident
Edwards, attended much to this ſubject, and wrote upon it more
than any other divine in this century.  In the year 1747, he
publiſhed a book, entitled " An humble attempt to promote ex-
plicit

plicit agreement, and vifible union of God's people, in extraordinary prayer for the revival of religion, and the advancement of Chrift's kingdom on earth, purfuant to fcripture promifes and prophecies concerning the laft time." In which he produces the evidence from fcripture, that fuch a day is yet to come. And in a pofthumous publication of his, intitled "A hiftory of the work of Redemption," this fubject is brought into view, and particularly confidered. There is alfo extant, a fermon on the Millennium, by the late Dr. Bellamy. And other writers have occafionally mentioned it. And this fubject appears to be brought more particularly into view in the public prayers and preaching, and in converfation, in this age, than in former times ; and the doctrine of the Millennium is more generally believed, and better underftood.

This is rather an encouragement to attempt farther to explain and illuftrate, this important, pleafing, ufeful fubject, in which every chriftian is fo much interefted, than a reafon why nothing more fhould be faid upon it. The fubject is far from being exhaufted ; and as the church advances nearer to the Millennium ftate, we have reafon to think the predictions in divine revelation refpecting it, will be better underftood ; and the minds of chriftians will be more excited to great attention to this fubject, and ftrong defires to look into thofe things, and to earneft longings and prayers for the coming of the kingdom of Chrift, as it will take place in that day. And all this is to be effected, by means and proper attempts and exertions. " Many fhall run to and fro, and knowledge fhall be increafed."

The prophecies of events which are yet to take place, cannot be fo fully underftood before thefe events come to pafs, as they will be when they are fulfilled ; and there is great danger of making miftakes about them. And it is certain, that many have made miftakes, fince they have made very different and oppofite conftructions of the fame predictions ; and therefore all cannot be right. So far as the prophecies which refpect the Millennium, of which there are many, can be underftood, and the real meaning of them be made plain, by a careful and diligent attention to them, and comparing them with each other, men may go on fafe ground, and be certain of their accomplifhment. And whatever is a plain and undeniable confequence, from what is exprefsly predicted, is equally revealed in the prediction, as an event, or cir-

eumftance

cumftance of an event, neceffarily included in it. But every opinion refpecting future events, which is matter of conjecture only, however probable it may be in the view of him who propofes it, ought to be entertained with modefty and diffidence.

The following treatife on the Millennium, is not defigned fo much to advance any new fentiments concerning it, which have never before been offered to the public, as to revive and repeat thofe which have been already fuggefted by fome authors, which are thought to be very important, and ought to be underftood, and kept conftantly in the view of all, in order to their having a proper conception of the church of Chrift in this world, and reading the fcriptures to their beft advantage, and greateft comfort: Though perhaps fomething will be advanced, refpecting the events which, according to fcripture, are to take place between the prefent time, and the introduction of the happy ftate of the church, which have not been before fo particularly confidered.

SECTION

# SECTION I.

*In which it is proved from Scripture, that the church
of Christ is to come to a state of prosperity in this world,
which it has never yet enjoyed ; in which it will continue at least a thousand years.*

T H E first revelation of a Redeemer, in the prediction
spoken to the serpent, may be considered as implying the destruction of the kingdom of the devil in this world, by the wisdom and
energy of Christ. " He shall bruise thy head, and thou shalt
bruise his heal."\* Satan has bruised the heal of Christ, in the
sufferings and dishonour he has been instrumental of bringing
upon him, and in the opposition he has made to the interest and
church of Christ, in this world. And it is natural to suppose,
that Christ shall bruise his head in this world, by destroying his
interest and kingdom among men, and gaining a conquest over
him, in the struggle and war which has taken place between the
Redeemer and seducer of men. And by the Redeemer's *bruising
the head* of the serpent, is signified that he will not destroy him
by the mere exertion of his power, but that by his superiour wisdom, he will confound and defeat satan, in all his subtilty and
cunning, on which he depends so much, and by which he aims
to disappoint Christ, and defeat him in his designs. And by this
he will make a glorious display of his wisdom, as well as of his
power, while he discovers the craftiness of satan to be foolishness,
and disappoints him in his devices, carrying all the counsel of this
cunning froward enemy headlong. If all this could not be
gathered from this passage, considered by itself ; yet that this is
the real meaning, will perhaps appear, from what has already
taken place in accomplishing this prediction ; and from other
prophecies respecting this, some of which are to be brought into
view in the sequel : Without which the full meaning of this first
promise could not be known.

B

In

\* Gen. iii. 15.

In order to bruife the head of the ferpent, in this fenfe, moft effectually ; and turn his boafted wifdom nnd cunning into fool-ifhnefs, and entirely defeat him in this way, he muft have opportunity and advantage to try his fkill and power, and practife all his cunning, in oppofing Chrift, and the falvation of men. And in this way be overcome and wholly defeated, in the ruin of his intereft and kingdom among men ; fo that all his attempts fhall turn againft himfelf, and be the occafion of making the victory and triumph of the Redeemer greater, more perfpicuous and glorious, in the final prevalence of his kingdom on earth, by drawing all men to him ; and deftroying the works and kingdom of fatan in this world, and fetting up his own on the ruins of it, and fo as to turn all the attempts and works of the devil againft him, and render the whole fubfervient to his own intereft and kingdom. And thus the coming and kingdom of Chrift will be, " As the light of the morning, when the fun rifeth, even a morning without clouds ; as the tender grafs fpringing out of the earth by clear fhining after rain." When the fun rifes in a clear morning, after a dark night, attended with clouds, rain and ftorms, the morning is more pleafant, beautiful and glorious, and the grafs fprings and grows more frefh and thrifty, than if it had not been preceded by fuch a ftormy night. So the profperity and glory of the church, when the fun of righteoufnefs fhall rife upon it, with healing in his beams, will be enjoyed to a higher degree, and be more pleafant and glorious, and Chrift will be more glorified, than if it had not been preceded by a dreadful night of darknefs, confufion and evil, by the wickednefs of men, and the power and agency of fatan.

The words above cited, are the laft words of David the Prophet, and fweet Pfalmift of Ifrael, and are a prophecy of the glorious event now under confideration. " The Spirit of the Lord fpake by me, and his word was in my tongue. The God of Ifrael faid, the Rock of Ifrael fpake by me. He that ruleth over men muft be juft, ruling in the fear of God. And he fhall be like the morning, when the fun rifeth, even a morning without clouds ; as the tender grafs fpringing out of the earth, by clear fhining after rain."* The firft words may be rendered fo as to give the true fenfe more clearly. " He who is to rule over men (i. e. the Meffiah) is juft, ruling in the fear of God." The words *muft be,*

in

* 2 Sam. xxiii. 2, 3, 4.

in our tranflation, are not in the original, and the helping verb *ɪ̀s*, which is commonly not expreffed, but underſtood, in the Hebrew, ſhould have been ſupplied ; " He that ruleth, or is to rule over men, *is* juſt." This is evidently a prophecy concerning Chriſt, his church and kingdom, when he ſhall take to himſelf his great power, and reign in his kingdom, which ſhall ſucceed the reign of ſatan during the four preceding monarchies, which were firſt to take place, which will be more particularly explained, as we proceed in examining the prophecies of this great event, *The latter day glory.* And that theſe words of David, are a prediction of the reign of Chriſt on earth, after the long prevalence of ſatan and wicked men, is farther evident from the words which follow, relative to the ſame thing. " But the ſons of Belial ſhall *all of them* as thorns be thurſt away, becauſe they cannot be taken with hands. But the man that ſhall touch them, muſt be fenced with iron, and the ſtaff of a ſpear, and they ſhall be utterly burnt with fire in the ſame place."

Exactly parallel with this prophecy, is that of the Prophet Malichi. " Behold, the day cometh, that ſhall burn as an oven, and all the proud, yea, all that do wickedly, ſhall be ſtubble, and the day that cometh ſhall burn them up, ſaith the Lord of hoſts, that it ſhall leave them neither root nor branch. But unto you that fear my name, ſhall the ſun of righteouſneſs ariſe with healing in his wings ; and ye ſhall go forth and grow up as the calves in the ſtall. And ye ſhall tread down the wicked ; for they ſhall be aſhes under the ſoles of your feet, in the day that I ſhall do this, ſaith the Lord of hoſts."*

But to return from this, which may ſeem to be ſome digreſſion, or anticipation : The great and remarkable promiſe, ſo often made to Abraham, Iſaac and Jacob, and more than once mentioned by the Apoſtles, will next be conſidered. This promiſe was made to Abraham, and of him, three times. " In thee ſhall all the families of the earth be bleſſed."† " All the nations of the earth ſhall be bleſſed in him"‡ " And in thy ſeed ſhall the nations of the earth be bleſſed."§ And this ſame promiſe is made to Iſaac. " I will perform the oath which I ſware unto Abraham thy father—and in thy ſeed ſhall all the nations of the earth be bleſſed."‖ And to Jacob. " In thee and in thy ſeed, ſhall all the families of the earth be

B 2                                                              be

* Mal. iv. 1, 2, 3.        † Gen. xii. 3.        ‡ Chap. xviii. 18.
§ Chap. xxii. 18.          ‖ Chap. xxvi. 4.

be bleffed."* The Apoftle Peter mentions this promife as referring to the days of the gofpel. "Ye are the children of the
Prophets, and of the covenant which God made with our fathers,
faying unto Abraham, And in thy feed fhall all the kindreds of the
earth be bleffed."† The Apoftle Paul fpeaks of this promife as
referring to Chrift, and all who believe in him, making ,him to
be the promifed feed, and believers in him to be thofe exclufively
who are bleffed in him, in whom the promifed good takes place.
"Know ye therefore, that they which are of faith, the fame are
the children of Abraham. And the fcripture, forefeeing that God
would juftify the heathen through faith, preached before the gofpel
unto Abraham, faying, In thee fhall all nations be bleffed. So
then they which be of faith, are bleffed with faithful Abraham.—
Now to Abraham and his feed were the promifes made. He faith
not, And to feeds, as of many; but as of one, And to thy feed,
which is Chrift."‡

This prediction and promife is very exprefs and extenfive, That
all the families, kindreds and nations of the earth, fhould be bleffed
in Chrift, by their becoming believers in him. This has never
yet taken place and cannot be fulfilled, unlefs chriftianity and the
kingdom of Chrift fhall take place and prevail in the world to a
vaftly higher degree, and more extenfively and univerfally, than
has yet come to pafs ; and all nations, all the inhabitants of the
earth, fhall become believers in him, agreeable to a great number
of other prophecies, fome of which will be mentioned in this
fection.

The reign of Chrift on earth, with his church and people, and
the happinefs and glory of that time, is a fubject often mentioned,
predicted and celebrated in the book of Pfalms. To mention all
that is there fpoken with reference to that happy time, would be
to tranfcribe great part of that book. Only the following paffages
will now be mentioned, which are thought abundantly to prove
that the kingdom of Chrift is to prevail and flourifh in this world,
as it has never yet done ; and the church is to be brought to a
ftate of purity, profperity and happinefs on earth, which has not
yet taken place, and fo as to include all nations, and fill the world.

In the fecond Pfalm, it is predicted and promifed, that the Son
of God fhall inherit and poffefs all nations, to the ends of the
earth ; which neceffarily implies, that his church and kingdom
                                                          fhall

* Chap. xxviii. 14.       † Acts iii. 25.       ‡ Gal. iii. 7, 8, 9, 16.

fhall be thus extenfive, reaching to the ends of the earth, and including all the nations and men on earth. "I have fet my king upon my holy hill of Zion. I will declare the decree : The Lord hath faid unto me, Thou art my Son, this day have I begotten thee. Afk of me, and I fhall give thee the heathen for thine inheritance, and the uttermoft parts of the earth for thy poffeffion." By Zion here is meant, as in numerous other places in the prophecies, the church of Chrift, of which Mount Zion was a type.

The twenty fecond Pfalm contains a prophecy of the fufferings of Chrift ; and the glory that fhall follow ; and of the latter it is faid ; " The meek fhall eat and be fatisfied. They fhall praife the Lord that feek him : Your heart fhall live forever. All the ends of the world fhall remember, and turn unto the Lord : And all the kindreds of the nations fhall worfhip before .thee. For the kingdom is the Lord's ; and he is the Governor among the nations : For evil doers fhall be cut off : But thofe that wait upon the Lord, they fhall inherit the earth, For yet a little while, and the wicked fhall not be ; yea, thou fhalt diligently confider his place, and it fhall not be. But the meek fhall inherit the earth, and delight themfelves in the abundance of peace."* This is a prediction of an event which has never taken place yet. Evil doers and the wicked, have in all ages hitherto poffeffed the earth, and flourifhed and reigned in the world. When it is promifed, that they who wait upon the Lord, and the meek fhall inherit the earth, and delight themfelves in the abundance of peace, the meaning muft be, that perfons of this character will yet have the poffeffion of the earth, and fill the world, when no place fhall be found for the wicked, as they fhall be all deftroyed, and their caufe wholly loft. And all of this character who have lived before this time, and waited upon the Lord in the exercife of meeknefs, fhall flourifh and live in their fucceffors, and in the profperity and triumph of the caufe and intereft, in which they lived and died. This is agreeable to other prophecies of this kind, as will be fhewn in the fequel. " All the ends of the earth fhall remember and turn unto the Lord : And all the kindreds of the nations fhall worfhip before thee·" Who can believe that this has ever yet been ? But few of mankind, compared with the whole, have yet turned unto the Lord. By far the greateft part of the nations of the earth, even to the ends of the world, have worfhipped and do

now

* Pfal. xxxvii. 9, 10, 11.

now worship falfe gods, and idols.   But when *all the ends of the
world* fhall remember, and turn to the Lord ;  and all the kindreds
of the nations fhall worfhip before him ;  then the meek fhall inherit the earth, and delight themfelves in the abundance of peace.

The whole of the fixty feventh Pfalm is a prediction of the fame
event, and of the fame time, which is yet to come.   It is a prayer
of the church that fuch a time may take place; at the fame time
expreffing her affurance that it was coming ;  and the whole is a
prophecy of it.   " God be merciful unto us, and blefs us ;  and
caufe his face to fhine upon us.   That thy way may be known
upon earth, thy faving health among *all nations.*   Let the people
praife thee, O God; let *all the people* praife thee.   O let the nations be glad, and fing for joy ;  for thou fhalt judge the people
righteoufly, and govern the nations upon earth.   Then fhall the
earth yield her increafe ;  and God, even our God, fhall blefs us.
God fhall blefs us ;  and *all the ends of the earth fhall fear him.*"

The feventy fecond Pfalm, the title of which is, " A Pfalm for
Solomon," contains a prophecy of Chrift and his kingdom, of
whom Solomon was an eminent type.   The Pfalmift looks beyond
the type to the antitype, and fays things which can be applied to
the latter only, and are not true of the former, confidered as dif-
tinct from the latter ;  which is common in the fcripture, in fuch
cafes.   Here it is faid, " He fhall come down like rain upon the
mown grafs ;  as fhowers that water the earth.   In his days fhall
the righteous flourifh ;  and abundance of peace fo long as the
moon endureth.   He fhall have dominion alfo from fea to fea,
and from the river unto the ends of the earth.   All kings fhall
fall down before him :  All nations fhall ferve him.   His name
fhall endure forever :  His name fhall be continued as long as the
fun and moon fhall be bleffed in him :  All nations fhall call him
bleffed.   Bleffed be the Lord God, the God of Ifrael, who only
doth wondrous things.   And bleffed be his glorious name forever, and let the whole earth be filled with his glory ;  Amen,
and Amen."

" Arife, O God, judge the earth ;  for thou fhalt inherit all
nations."*   In this Pfalm, the rulers and judges among men are
accufed of unrighteoufnefs, and condemned ;  and then the Pfalmift concludes with the words now quoted, which refer to fome
future event, in which God fhould judge the earth, and inherit
all

* Pfal. lxxxii. 8.

all nations, in a fenfe in which he had not yet done it. In the fecond Pfalm, the heathen, i. e. the nations, all nations, are given to Chrift for his inheritance ; and here the fame thing is ex-preffed, " Thou fhalt inherit all nations." And by his *judging the earth*, is meant his reigning and fubduing the inhabitants of the earth, to a cordial fubjection to himfelf; which will be more evident by what follows, where we fhall find the fame thing pre-dicted.

The ninety fixth Pfalm, relates wholly to redemption by Chrift ; to the happinefs and glory of his kingdom, and his reign on earth. " O worfhip the Lord in the beauty of holinefs : *Fear before him, all the earth.* Say among the heathen, that the Lord reigneth : The world alfo fhall be eftablifhed, that it fhall not be moved, he fhall judge the people righteoufly. Let the heavens re-joice, and let the earth be glad : Let the fea roar, and the fulnefs thereof. Let the field be joyful, and all that is there-in : Then fhall all the trees of the wood rejoice before the Lord ; for he cometh to judge the earth : He fhall judge the world with righteoufnefs, and the people with his truth." What is here foretold, is to take place before the end of the world, and the general judgment ; and it relates to the whole world, all the earth and the nations in it ; the kingdom and reign of Chrift is to extend to all of them : And his coming to judge the earth, and the world in righteoufnefs, intends his reigning in righteoufnefs, and bringing all nations to fhare in the bleffings of his falvation and kingdom. Agreeable to this, it is faid by Chrift, by Ifaiah and Jeremiah, " Behold a king fhall reign *in righteoufnefs.* In thofe days, and at that time, will I caufe the branch of righteouf-nefs to grow up unto David, and he fhall execute *judgment and righteoufnefs* in the land," or in the earth.*

Great part of the prophecy of Ifaiah, relates to the flourifhing and happy ftate of the kingdom of Chrift, and the profperity of the church in the latter days. When he foretells the return of the people of Ifrael from the Babylonifh captivity, which was a type of the deliverance of the church of Chrift from fpiritual Ba-bylon, and from all her enemies in this world, vifible and invifi-ble, he commonly looks forward to the latter, and keeps that in view, and fays things of it, which are not true of the former, and cannot be applied to it. And as Zion, Jerufalem, and Judah, and Ifrael,

* Ifai. xxxii. 1. Jer. xxxiii. 15.

Ifrael, were types of the church and kingdom of Chrift, as including all nations, the former are commonly mentioned only as types,
being put for, and fygnifying the latter.    And when the gofpel
day, the coming of Chrift, and his church and kingdom, are
brought into view, all that is included in thefe is comprehended;
and commonly chief reference is had to the Millennium, or the
day of the flourifhing of the kingdom of Chrift on earth, which is
in a peculiar manner, and eminently the day of falvation ; and
will iffue in the complete redemption of the church, at and after
the day of judgment.    He who reads this prophecy with care and
difcerning, will be convinced of the truth of thefe obfervations;
and in any other view, great part of it cannot be underftood.

Only part of the many prophecies of the glory and extent of
the kingdom of Chrift in this world, which are contained in this
book, will be now mentioned, as thofe which are moft exprefs and
clear, with reference to the fubject in view.    They who attentive-
ly read this prophecy, will find many more which refer to the
fame event.

" And it fhall come to pafs in the laft days, that the mountain
of the Lord's houfe fhall be eftablifhed in the top of the mountains,
and fhall be exalted above the hills ; and all nations fhall flow
unto it.    And many people fhall go and fay, Come ye, and let us
go up to the mountain of the Lord, to the houfe of the God of
Jacob, and he will teach us of his ways, and we will walk in his
paths ; for out of Zion fhall go forth the law, and the word of
the Lord from Jerufalem.    And he fhall judge among the nations,
and fhall rebuke many people : And they fhall beat their fwords
into plowfhares, and their fpears into pruning hooks : Nation
fhall not lift up fword againft nation, neither fhall they learn war
any more."*    It is certain, that this prophecy has not been yet
fulfilled, except in a very fmall degree, as the beginning, and firft
fruits of it.

" And there fhall come forth a rod out of the ftem of Jeffe, and
a branch fhall grow out of his roots.    And the Spirit of the Lord
fhall reft upon him, the fpirit of wifdom and underftanding, the
fpirit of knowledge, and of the fear of the Lord : And fhall make
him of quick underftanding in the fear of the Lord, and he fhall
not judge after the fight of his eyes, neither reprove after the hear-
ing of his ears.    But with righteoufnefs fhall he judge the poor,

                                                          and

* Ifai. ii. 2, 3, 4.

and reprove with equity, for the meek of the earth : And he fhall fmite the earth with the rod of his mouth, and with the breath of his lips fhall he flay the wicked. And righteoufnefs fhall be the girdle of his loins, and faithfulnefs the girdle of his reins. The wolf alfo fhall dwell with the lamb, and the leopard fhall lie down with the kid ; and the calf, and the young lion, and the fatling together, and a little child fhall lead them. And the cow and the bear fhall feed ; their young ones fhall lie down together : And the lion fhall eat ftraw like the ox. The fucking child fhall play on the hole of the afp, and the weaned child fhall put his hand on the cockatrice' den. They fhall not hurt nor deftroy in all my holy mountain : For the earth fhall be full of the knowledge of the Lord, as the waters cover the fea.''*

This is evidently a prophecy of Chrift, and his kingdom on earth. He fhall judge and reprove for the meek of the earth, and flay all the wicked on earth, that the meek may inherit it; which is exactly agreeable to the forementioned prophecy in the thirty feventh Pfalm. " Evil doers fhall be cut off, and yet a little while and the wicked fhall not be ; but the meek fhall inherit the earth ; and delight themfelves in the abundance of peace." And this univerfal peace and harmony among men, which fhall take place at that time, is expreffed in the prophecy before us, in very ftrong, figurative language ; by the wolf dwelling with the lamb, &c.— And the ground and reafon of this is given. " For the earth fhall be full of the knowledge of the Lord, as the waters cover the fea." By the knowledge of the Lord is meant true religion, or real chriftianity, which confifts moft effentially in benevolence and goodnefs, as has been fhown. So far as this takes place, love, peace, and the moft happy concord and union, are promoted ; and every thing contrary to this fuppreffed and banifhed. Therefore, when this fhall take place univerfally among men, and fill the earth, as the waters cover the fea, there will be nothing to deftroy or hurt, but univerfal fafety, peace and love. No fuch time has ever been yet known. The true knowledge of God has been fo far from filling the earth ; that grofs darknefs has covered much the greateft part of it ; and real chriftianity has been confined to narrow bounds ; and but very few of mankind have attained to the character of true chriftians, even where the gofpel has been publifhed. And a horrible fcene of oppreffion, cruelty, war and murder, has

fpread

* Chap. xi. 1—9.

spread all over the earth ; and will continue to do so, until Christ
shall arise and smite the earth with the rod of his mouth, and slay
the wicked with the breath of his lips ; and cause the earth to be
filled with the knowledge of God.   Such a happy time is yet
future, and will certainly come.

The twenty fifth chapter contains a prophecy of the same event,
some of which is worthy to be transcribed.   "And in this mountain, shall the Lord of hosts make unto *all people* a feast of fat things,
a feast of wine on the lees, of fat things full of marrow, of wines
on the lees well refined.   And he will destroy in this mountain
the face of the covering cast over *all people*, and the vail that is
spread over *all nations*.   He will swallow up death in victory, and
the Lord God will wipe away tears from off all faces, and the rebuke of his people shall he take away from off all the earth ; for
the Lord hath spoken it.   And it shall be said in that day, Lo, this
is our God, we have waited for him, and he will save us : This is
the Lord, we have waited for him, we will be glad, and rejoice
in his salvation."

The gospel is here represented by a rich feast ; and it is promised
that all people and nations shall have their eyes opened to see it ;
and all reproach, and opposition to the church of Christ, shall be
taken away from off all the earth ; and there shall be universal
joy in the salvation, for which the church has long waited, and
which shall come in the last day.

"Comfort ye, comfort ye my people, saith your God.   Speak
comfortably to Jerusalem, and cry unto her, that her warfare is
accomplished, that her iniquity is pardoned : For she hath received of the Lord's hand double for all her sins.   The voice of him
that crieth in the wilderness, Prepare ye the way of the Lord, make
straight in the desert a high way for our God.   Every valley shall
be exalted, and every mountain and hill shall be made low ; and
the crooked shall be made straight, and the rough places plain.
And the glory of the Lord shall be revealed, and *all flesh shall see it
together* : For the mouth of the Lord hath spoken it."*

This is a prophecy of the times of the gospel, as it is thus applied in the New Testament.   It does refer to the first introduction and the coming of Christ into the world ; but is not confined
to this : It gives a comprehensive view of this great salvation, and
the favour and glory which is to come to the church of Christ in
                                                          this

* Isai. xl. 1, &c.

this world, and looks forward to the day, when the glory of the Lord shall be so revealed that all flesh, that is, all nations, all mankind, shall see it together. This has not yet been fulfilled ; but is to be accomplished in a time yet to come, when " The earth shall be filled with the knowledge of the glory of the Lord, as the waters cover the sea."\* All that precedes this day is preparatory to it, as the ministry of John the baptist, was an introduction to it, and more immediately prepared the way for Christ.

From the beginning of the fortieth chapter of Isaiah, to the end of the sixty sixth chapter, with which his prophecy closes, there is almost one continued series of predictions and promises of good, salvation, happiness and glory to the church of Christ, which have principal reference to the latter day when the Millennium shall take place ; and when they will have their chief accomplishment. It will be sufficient to answer the end now proposed, to mention the following passages.

Salvation by Christ, is frequently represented as actually extended *to the ends of the earth*, which has not yet been accomplished. " Look unto me, and be ye saved, *all the ends of the earth* ; for I am God, and there is none else. And he said, It is a light thing that thou shouldest be my servant to raise up the tribes of Jacob, and to restore the preserved of Israel : I will also give thee for a light to the Gentiles, that thou mayst be my salvation *unto the end of the earth.* The Lord hath made bare his holy arm in the eyes of *all nations*, and *all the ends of the earth* shall see the salvation of our God."† The same phrase is used by the prophet Micah. " And he shall stand and feed in the strength of the Lord, in the majesty of the name of the Lord his God, and they shall abide : For now shall he be great *unto the ends of the earth.*"‡

The sixtieth chapter of Isaiah, is filled with comfort and promises to the church, as also are the preceding chapters. The following expressions may be particularly noted. " Arise, shine, for thy light is come, and the glory of the Lord is risen upon thee. For behold the darkness shall cover the earth, and gross darkness the people ; but the Lord shall arise upon thee, and his glory shall be seen upon thee. The Gentiles shall come to thy light, and kings to thy rising. Therefore, thy gates shall be open continually, they shall not be shut day nor night, that men may bring unto thee the forces of the Gentiles, and that their kings may be

B 2                                    brought.

\* Hab. ii. 14.    † Isai. xlv. 22. xlix. 6. lii. 10.    ‡ Chap. v. 4.

brought. For the nation and kingdom that will not fer e thee shall perish : Yea, those nations shall be utterly wasted." No such event has been yet. When this shall take place, all nations, all mankind, must belong to the church ; for all others shall be *utterly wasted.* The same thing is foretold by the Prophet Zechariah.*

The sixty first chapter of Isaiah, is on the same subject, and the sixty second throughout. Upon such promises made to the church, she breaks forth into joy and praise, in the prospect of the good that is coming to her. " I will greatly rejoice in the Lord, my soul shall be joyful in my God ; for he hath clothed me with the garments of salvation ; he hath covered me with the robe of righteousness, as a bridegroom decketh himself with ornaments, and as a bride adorneth herself with jewels. For as the earth bringeth forth her bud, and as the garden causeth the things that are sown in it to spring forth ; so the Lord God will cause righteousness and praise to spring forth *before all nations.*" " For Zion's sake, I will not hold my peace, and for Jerusalem's sake, I will not rest, until the righteousness thereof go forth as brightness, and the salvation thereof as a lamp that burneth. And the Gentiles shall see thy righteousness, and all kings thy glory : And thou shalt be called by a new name, which the mouth of the Lord shall name. I have set watchmen upon thy walls, O Jerusalem, which shall never hold their peace day nor night. Ye that make mention of the Lord, keep not silence, and give him no rest, till he establish, and till he make Jerusalem *a praise in the earth.* Go through, go through the gates ; prepare you the way of the people ; cast up, cast up the highway, gather out the stones, lift up a standard for the people. Behold, the Lord hath proclaimed *unto the end of the world,* Say ye to the daughter of Zion, Behold, thy salvation cometh ; behold, his reward is with him, and his work before him. And they shall call them, The holy people, the redeemed of the Lord : And thou shalt be called, Sought out, A city not forsaken."† " Who hath heard such a thing ? Who hath seen such things ? Shall the earth be made to bring forth in one day, or shall a nation be born at once ? For as soon as Zion travailed, she brought forth her children. Shall I bring to the birth, and not cause to bring forth ? saith the Lord. Shall I cause to bring forth, and shut the womb ? saith thy God. Rejoice ye with Jerusalem, and be glad with her,

all

* Chap. iii. 14—19.　　† Chap. lxii. 1, 2; 6, 7, 10, 11, 12.

all ye that love her ; rejoice for joy with her, all ye that mourn for her': That ye may fuck, and be fatisfied with the breafts of her confolations ; that ye may milk out, and be delighted with the abundance of her glory. For thus faith the Lord, Behold, I will extend peace to her like a river, and the glory of the Gentiles like a flowing ftream."*

In the prophecy of Jeremiah, the following paffages are found, which predict the utter abolition of idolatry on earth, and the converfion of all nations to chriftianity, which events have not yet come to pafs. " At that time they fhall call Jerufalem (i. e. the church) the throne of the Lord (i. e. The Lord fhall reign in and by it.) And all nations fhall be gathered unto it, to the name of the Lord, to Jerufalem ; (i. e. fhall become members of the church.) Neither fhall they walk any more after the imagination of their evil heart."† They fhall wholly renounce their idolatry, and all their wickednefs. " Thus fhall ye fay unto them, The gods that have not made the heavens and the earth, even they fhall perifh from the earth, and from under thofe heavens. They are vanity, and the work of errors. In the time of their vifitation they fhall perifh."‡ According to this prophecy, this will take place while this earth and the heavens remain, and therefore before the day of judgment.

This fubject is fet in a very clear light in the book of Daniel the Prophet. It is there repeatedly declared that the church, or kingdom of Chrift, fhall be the laft kingdom on earth ; that' it fhall fucceed four preceding monarchies, become great, and fill the world, and exift in a very happy and glorious ftate on earth. By the dream of Nebuchadnezzar, and the interpretation of it in the fecond chapter of Daniel, the kingdom of Chrift is fet in this light. The image which Nebuchadnezzar faw, reprefents four kingdoms or monarchies, viz. 1. The Babylonian. 2. The Medo Perfian, or that of the Medes and Perfians. 3. The Macedonian or Grecian. 4. The Roman. Thefe are all to pafs away and be deftroyed, to make way for a fifth kingdom, which fhall be great, and fill the world ; which is defcribed in the dream, by the following words : " Thou faweft till a ftone was cut out without hands, which fmote the image upon his feet that were of iron and clay, and break them in pieces. Then were the iron, the clay, the

* Chap. lxvi. 8, 9, 10, 11, 12. † Chap. iii. 17. ‡ Chap. x. 11, 15.

the brafs, the filver and gold, broken to pieces together, and became like the chaff of the fummer threfhing floors, and the wind carried them away, that no place was found for them : And the ftone that fmote the image became a great mountain, and *filled the whole earth.* This is interpreted by Daniel in the following words : " And in the days of thefe kings fhall the God of heaven fet up a kingdom, which fhall never be deftroyed : And the kingdom fhall not be left to other people, but it fhall break in pieces, and confume all thefe kingdoms, and it fhall ftand forever. For as much as thou faweft that the ftone was cut out of the mountain without hands, and that it broke in pieces the iron, the brafs, the clay, the filver and gold, the great God hath made known to the king what fhall come to pafs hereafter." That this laft kingdom is the kingdom of Chrift, there can be no doubt.* The fame is called in the New Teftament, " The kingdom of God, or the kingdom of heaven." This is to fucceed the kingdom of the Romans, and to fill the whole earth, in which all nations, all mankind will be included. The Roman empire or kingdom, is not yet wholly deftroyed ; therefore what is here predicted of the kingdom of Chrift is not yet accomplifhed, but fhall take place in fome future day. Nothing can be plainer and more certain than this.

In the feventh chapter of this book there is a reprefentation of the fame thing in a vifion which Daniel had. He faw the fame four empires or kingdoms in their fucceffion, reprefented by four great, wild, fierce beafts, coming up from the fea. The laft kingdom turned into a little horn which came up laft ; and Daniel " beheld till this fourth beaft with the little horn was flain, and his body deftroyed, and given to the burning flame." And then the vifion proceeds, " I faw in the night vifions, and beheld, one like the Son of man, come with the clouds of heaven, and came to the ancient of days, and they brought him near before him. And there was given him dominion, and glory, and a kingdom, that all people, nations, and languages fhould ferve him : His dominion is an everlafting dominion, which fhall not pafs away, and his kingdom that which fhall not be deftroyed." This vifion is briefly explained to Daniel in the following words: " Thefe great beafts, which are four, are four kings (i. e. kingdoms) which fhall arife out of the earth. But the faints of the Moft High fhall take the kingdom, and poffefs the kingdom forever, even for-

ever

* See Newton on the Prophecies, vol. I. p. 426, 427, &c.

ever and ever." Daniel requefted a more particular explanation of the fourth beaft, and of the ten horns, and of the little horn, " Even of that horn that had eyes, and a mouth that fpake very great things, whofe look was more ftout than his fellows. And the fame horn made war with the faints and prevailed againft them; until the ancient of days came, and judgment was given to the faints of the Moft High; and the time came that the faints poffeffed the kingdom." And he is then told, " That the fourth beaft fhall be the fourth kingdom upon earth. And the ten horns out of this kingdom, are ten kings that fhall arife : And another fhall rife after them, and he fhall be diverfe from the firft, and he fhall fubdue three kings. And he fhall fpeak great words againft the Moft High, and fhall wear out the faints of the Moft High, and think to change times and laws : And they fhall be given into his hand, until a time, and times, and the dividing of time. But the judgment fhall fit, and they fhall take away his dominion, to confume and to deftroy it to the end. *And the kingdom and dominion, and the greatnefs of the kingdom under the whole heaven, fhall be given to the people of the faints of the Moft High,* whofe kingdom is an everlafting kingdom, and all dominions fhall ferve and obey him."

As in Nebuchadnezzar's dream, fo in this vifion, the fifth and laft kingdom, is the kingdom of Chrift, confifting wholly of faints. It is Jefus Chrift whom Daniel faw, " And behold, one like to the Son of man came with the clouds of heaven. And there was given him dominion and glory, and a kingdom, that all people, nations and languages fhould ferve him." His kingdom and dominion is univerfal, including all the inhabitants of the earth. And thefe fhall be all faints or holy perfons; as no others can be the proper fubjects of this kingdom. " The faints of the Moft High fhall take the kingdom, and poffefs the kingdom forever. And the kingdom, and dominion, and the greatnefs of the kingdom under the whole heaven, fhall be given to the people of the faints of the Moft High." The ftrongeft expreffions are ufed and repeated, to affert the univerfality of this kingdom, comprehending all mankind who fhall then live on earth. And it is repeatedly declared, that this kingdom fhall ftand forever. It fhall not be deftroyed by any fucceeding power or kingdom, as the former kingdoms were, but fhall continue to the end of the world, and then be removed to heaven, to a more perfect and glorious ftate; and there exift and flourifh in the higheft perfection forever and ever. The

The little horn which was on the beaſt, and deſtroyed with the beaſt, whoſe body was given to the burning flame, is the Pope of Rome, with the kingdom and power, civil and eccleſiaſtical, of which he is the head.* This beaſt with this horn, is not yet deſtroyed. When this is done, the kingdom and power of ſin and ſatan in the world will fall; and then the kingdom of Chriſt will riſe and fill the world, as is predicted here, and in the ſecond chapter of this book. This is very evident by theſe prophecies, if there were no other; but this truth is greatly illuſtrated and eſtabliſhed, by thoſe predictions of the ſame event which have been conſidered; and more ſo, by thoſe which are yet to be mentioned.

The Prophet Micah predicted the proſperity of the church of Chriſt, and the prevalence of his intereſt and kingdom *in the laſt days*.† And there is a particular prophecy of the ſame event by Zephaniah.‡ This is alſo particularly foretold by Zechariah: " Sing and rejoice, O daughter of Zion, for lo, I come, and I will dwell in the midſt of thee, ſaith the Lord. And many nations ſhall be joined to the Lord in that day, and ſhall be my people; and I will dwell in the midſt of thee."§ Rejoice greatly, O daughter of Zion; ſhout, O daughter of Jeruſalem! Behold thy king cometh unto thee: He is juſt, and having ſalvation, lowly, and riding upon an aſs, and upon a colt the fole of an aſs. And I will cut off the chariot from Ephraim, and the horſe from Jeruſalem, and the battle bow ſhall be cut off; and he ſhall ſpeak peace unto the heathen: *And his dominion ſhall be from ſea even to ſea, and from the river even to the ends of the earth.*‖ The whole of the fourteenth chapter relates chiefly to this great event, and happy time; of which only the following words will be tranſcribed. " And it ſhall come to paſs in that day, that the light ſhall not be clear, and dark. But it ſhall be *one day*, which ſhall be known to the Lord, not day and night: But it ſhall come to paſs, that at evening time it ſhall be light. And it ſhall be in that day, that living waters ſhall go out from Jeruſalem: Half of them toward the former ſea, and half of them toward the hinder ſea: In ſummer and in winter it ſhall be. And the Lord ſhall be king over all the earth. In that day there ſhall be one Lord, and his name one." This

---

. * This is abundantly proved in Newton's Diſſertation on the Prophecies, vol. I. page 441—498.            † Chap. iv. 1—4. v. 1—4.
‡ Chap. iii. 8, to the end of the chapter.      § Chap. ii. 10, 11.
‖ Chap. ix. 9, 10.

This is a prophecy of the Millennium state, in figurative language. Then, in the moral world, the church, there shall be no night or darkness ; no change of day and night, as there was before, when the church was in a state of affliction, when her days of prosperity were short, and soon succeeded by darkness and night of degeneracy and affliction : But at the time when night used to come on, it shall be day ; so that it shall be constantly light and day, and the enjoyment of prosperity, light and holiness, without interruption. And there shall be a constant flow of living waters, without any interruption, into all parts of the earth, among all nations ; that is spiritual blessings, consisting in spiritual life, holy joy and happiness. And then all idolatry and false worship shall be wholly abolished ; and Christ shall reign in all the earth, and all nations shall trust in him, and obey him. This prediction agrees exactly with all those which have been mentioned, pointing out the same important glorious event.

The prophecies in the New Testament, foretold the universal spread of christianity, until all nations shall become the servants of Christ ; and that Christ and his people shall reign on earth a thousand years ; when satan shall be cast out of the earth, and his subjects and kingdom shall be destroyed ; agreeable to the numerous prophecies in the Old Testament, which have been mentioned.

Jesus Christ has foretold this, by the following parables.— " Another parable put he forth unto them, saying, The kingdom of heaven is like to a grain of mustard seed, which a man took and sowed in his field. Which indeed is the least of all seeds : But when it is grown, it is the greatest among herbs, and becometh a tree ; so that the birds of the air come and lodge in the branches thereof. Another parable spake he unto them, The kingdom of heaven is like unto leaven, which a woman took and hid in three measures of meal, till the whole was leavened."* By the first of those parables Christ teaches, that his church and kingdom, though small in the beginning of it, should increase and become great in the world. In the next, he makes an advance, and more fully predicts the universal extent of this kingdom ; that the gospel shall not cease to spread and influence the world, till all mankind, living on earth, the whole world, shall be formed by it, and imbibe

* Matth. xiii. 31, 32, 33.

the spirit of it ; so as to become the children of this kingdom. If the kingdom of heaven shall not finally prevail and extend to all nations, and fill the whole world, how can this parable be a just or true representation of it ? In this view of it, it agrees exactly with many of the prophecies which have been mentioned ; and with others, which are yet to be considered.

Agreeable to this, are the following words of Christ, in which indeed he asserts the same thing, "Now is the judgment of this world : Now shall the prince of this world be cast out. And I, if I be lifted up from the earth, will draw all men unto me."*— What is here foretold by Christ, is not yet accomplished, except in a very small part, as the first fruits and pledge of the whole.— A foundation for this was laid in the death of Christ, when he was lifted up on the cross ; but the prince of this world, the devil, is not yet cast out of the world ; nor has Christ yet drawn all men unto him. Christ has drawn great numbers to him, who have become his faithful subjects and servants, and has made great inroads upon the interest and kingdom of the prince of this world ; but very few of mankind, compared with the whole, have been drawn to Christ ; by far the greatest number even in the christian world, have rejected and opposed him ; and the kingdom of satan has been great and strong, including the most of men who have lived in the world, from the time in which these words were spoken by Christ, to this day. Both of these events are therefore yet future, and the former is to make way for the latter ; or rather one is included in the other. The same things which are here foretold, are predicted in different words, in the twentieth chapter of the Revelation, which will be considered. When Christ says, He will draw *all men* unto him, he does not mean that every one of mankind shall come unto him ; for this is contrary to known fact ; and to many express declarations of Christ. But that in consequence of his death, the kingdom of satan shall be utterly destroyed on earth, and then all nations, even all men then in the world, shall become his voluntary subjects, and believe in him.

This was suited to support and comfort his disciples and friends at that time, when he had been speaking of his own death as at hand, in the view of the glory that should follow his dying on the cross : and served to explain what was spoken by the voice from

heaven,

* John xii. 31, 32.

heaven, in anfwer to his petition, " Father, glorify thy name."—
" I have both glorified it, and will glorify it again."*

What the Apoftle Paul fays in the eleventh chapter of his
epiftle to the Romans, of the Jews and Gentiles, which comprehend all mankind, holds forth this fame truth. He there fpeaks of
the Jews who were then, the moft of them, broken off from the
church by unbelief, as yet to come into the kingdom of Chrift, even
all of them, which he terms their *fulnefs.* And he fays, that when
they fhall in their fulnefs be brought in, the fulnefs of the Gentiles fhall come in alfo. The fulnefs of the Jews, and the fulnefs
of the Gentiles, muft include the whole of all nations. And he
fpeaks of what had taken place in the days of the Apoftles, in the
converfion of Jews and Gentiles, as only the firft fruits, the root,
foundation and beginning, of the whole lump, and the tree which
were to follow in the coming in of the Jews and Gentiles, of the
whole world, in the fulnefs thereof.†

This leads to recollect the many prophecies by the ancient
Prophets, of the reftoration of the Jews to a ftate of holinefs and
happinefs, in the laft days, which has not yet come to pafs, fome
of which it may be proper to mention here, as they ferve to confirm the point under confideration. The thirty fourth, thirty
fixth, and thirty feventh chapters of Ezekiel, relate chiefly to this
event. Though the return of the Jews from their captivity in
Babylon, may be implied in this prophecy, and fome expreffions
may have particular reference to that ; yet it evidently looks farther, to a deliverance and falvation, of which their return from
Babylon was a type or pledge : And there are many things predicted, which cannot be applied to the former, and were not true
of it. Particularly the following : " I will fet up one fhepherd
over them, and he fhall feed them, even my fervant David : And
he fhall feed them, and he fhall be their fhepherd. One king fhall
be king to them all. And I will cleanfe them, fo fhall they be my
people, and I will be their God. And David, my fervant, fhall
be king over them, and they all fhall have one fhepherd. They
fhall alfo walk in my judgments, and obferve my ftatutes, and do
them. And they fhall dwell in the land that I have given unto
Jacob my fervant, wherein your fathers have dwelt, and they fhall
dwell therein, even they and their children, and their childrens'

D 2                    children

children forever, and my fervant David, fhall be their prince forever."* By David, Jefus Chrift the Son of David is meant, as the former was an eminent type of the latter. Therefore this muft refer to their reftoration and happy ftate under Chrift, which is certainly not yet come ; but will take place, when there fhall be one fold, and one fhepherd, and Jews and Gentiles fhall be united in one church under the Redeemer, which, after the Millennium, fhall be tranfplanted from earth to heaven ; where the fpiritual David will reign over it forever.

The fame is foretold by the Prophet Hofea. " The children of Ifrael fhall abide many days without a king, and without a prince, and without a facrifice, and without an image, and without an ephod, and without teraphim. Afterward fhall the children of Ifrael return, and feek the Lord their God, and David their king, and fhall fear the Lord, and his goodnefs in the latter days."†— The children of Ifrael are now in the ftate here defcribed, without a king, and without a prince ; without a facrifice ; for their temple is deftroyed, and they cannot go to Jerufalem, and their law forbids them to facrifice in any other place. They are without an image, without an ephod and teraphim ; for they have a great and obftinate averfion from all kinds of idolatry, to which they were once fo much addicted. They have been a long time, many days, in this ftate, and will continue fo, until they return, and feek Jefus Chrift their king, and fubmit to him, which is yet to come.

Thefe prophecies, and others of the fame kind, if they be confidered as having reference to the Jews exclufively, and not including the whole church of Chrift, in the latter day, compofed of Jews and Gentiles, do prove that there is yet to be a time, when the church of Chrift fhall be univerfal, and include all nations : For it appears from what St. Paul fays, that when thofe prophecies fhall be fulfilled to the Jews, the fulnefs of the Gentiles will alfo come in, and all men in every nation will be fubject to Chrift, and his kingdom fhall be glorious, and fill the world. And in this fenfe " All Ifrael fhall be faved."

In the revelation made by Jefus Chrift to the Apoftle John, the final victory and triumph of the church on earth, over all her enemies, and the happy ftate to which it will be brought, which fhall

continue

* Chap. xxxiv. 23. xxxvii. 22, 23, 24, 25.      † Chap. iii. 4, 5.

continue a thoufand years, is, in fome refpects, more clearly fet forth, than in the preceding prophecies ; by which they are illuf-trated, and their meaning is more fully fixed and confirmed. Here the general ftate and circumftances of the church, from the time when the revelation was given, to this time, and down to the end of the world, are predicted. Here the afflictions and per-fecutions, through which the church fhould pafs ; the refpite which fhe fhould have, and victory over the perfecuting power of hea-then Rome, in the days of Conftantine; the grand apoftacy which fhould take place in the church by the rife of the Pope, and the hierarchy of the falfe church of Rome; the grofs idolatry which fhould be practifed in that church; and the violent oppofition of this power to the true followers of Chrift ; their cruel perfecutions of them, and fhedding their blood, for a thoufand two hundred and fixty years ; the judgments that fhould be executed on that corrupt church and her adherents, and on the whole world, for their obftinacy in wickednefs; and the final overthrow of the Pope and all who fupport him, and of the kingdom of fatan in the world, and the deliverance of the church of Chrift into a ftate of reft and peace, when this kingdom of Chrift fhall increafe and fpread, and fill the world ; and continue in this happy ftate on earth a thoufand years : All this is foretold ; much of which is already come to pafs; but the moft happy and glorious events are yet to come. The great and remarkable things which have come to pafs, as they were foretold, are a ftanding, inconteftible evidence and demonftration, that the prophecies in this book are from heaven : For it is as certain, that none but the omnifcient God can know and predict fuch events, which take place accord-ing to the prediction, as it is that this world was made by him. And the events which are come to pafs, and are now taking place in the world before our eyes, agreeable to the prophecies in this book, at the fame time that they prove that thofe predictions are from God, are alfo a pledge and affurance, that the prophecies of things not yet come, will be fulfilled in due feafon.

The fubject now in hand, will lead more particularly to con-fider what are the prophecies in this book, which relate to the future profperity of the church and kingdom of Chrift in this world, in which all the darknefs and afflictions which do attend it, being oppreffed and trodden down by enemies, while they prevail

and

and triumph, fhall iffue ; and to fhow that fuch a day is certainly
coming, according to the predictions which are to be found here.

In the fifth chapter of the Revelation, the four-and twenty
elders, who reprefent the church, appear rejoicing and praifing
Chrift in the profpect of their reigning on the earth. " And they
fung a new fong, faying, Thou art worthy to take the book, and
to open the feals thereof : For thou waft flain, and haft redeemed
us to God by thy blood, out of every kindred, and tongue, and
people, and nation ; and haft made us unto our God kings and
priefts : *And we fhall reign on the earth.*" This is fpoken of *the
church*, and is not literally true of every particular member of it,
that then actually exifted in heaven, or on earth. When the
church fhall reign on earth, confifting of the numerous members
who fhall then exift in this world ; all thofe who are gone out of
the world, and are in heaven, will reign in and with the church
on earth, as members of the fame fociety and kingdom ; and will
partake in all the joy and glory of this event, in a much higher degree than if they were perfonally on earth : They will reign in
their fucceffors, who reprefent them, and in the prevalence, victory
and triumph of that caufe, which is theirs, and in which they
lived and died. But this will be more particularly confidered
hereafter.

" And the feventh angel founded, and there were great voices
in heaven, faying, The kingdoms of this world are become the
kingdom of our Lord, and of his Chrift, and he fhall reign forever
and ever."* Here it is afferted, that under the feventh trumpet,
which contains all the events from the time of its founding, to
the end of the world, all the nations and kingdoms in this world
fhall become one kingdom, under Chrift, and fhall be wholly
fwallowed up in this kingdom, which fhall not be fucceeded or
give place to any other kingdom ; but fhall ftand forever. It
fhall continue the only kingdom on earth to the end of the world,
and exift forever in heaven. Which is perfectly agreeable to
many other prophecies which have been mentioned. The meaning is not, that this event fhall follow immediately upon the founding of the feventh trumpet ; but that this is comprehended in the
events of this trumpet, to which all the preceding have refpect,
and in which they fhall iffue, as the moft important and glorious
event,

* Chap. x. 15.

event, to which all the inhabitants of heaven were attending, and in the profpect of which they had peculiar joy.

The fame event is celebrated in heaven, as having actually taken place, in the former part of the nineteenth chapter. " And I heard as it were the voice of a great multitude, and as the voice of many waters, and as the voice of mighty thunderings, faying, Hallelujah ! for the Lord God omnipotent reigneth : Let us be glad and rejoice, and give honour to him ; for the marriage of the Lamb is come, and his wife hath made herfelf ready. And to her was granted, that fhe fhould be arrayed in fine linen, clean and white : For the fine linen is the righteoufnefs of faints. And he faid unto me, Write, Bleffed are they who are called unto the marriage fupper of the Lamb. And he faith unto me, Thefe are the true fayings of God." Here the Lord Jefus Chrift is reprefented as reigning, as he never had done before ; which is the fame event which is fo often predicted in the Pfalms, and by the Prophets, efpecially by Daniel, by the Lord's reigning, that is Chrift. And which is mentioned and celebrated in the tenth chapter ; and in the twentieth chapter ; " And I faw thrones, and they fat upon them, and judgment was given unto them, and they lived and reigned with Chrift a thoufand years." By the bride having made herfelf ready, and being arrayed in fine linen, clean and white, is meant the eminent degree of holinefs and moral beauty, to which the church will arrive at that day, in the Millennium ftate. This is reprefented as taking place upon the fall of antichrift, and the great whore, the falfe idolatrous church of Rome. And it fucceeds the overthrow of fatan's kingdom in the world, and not only the deftruction of the Roman empire under antichrift, but of all the nations of wicked men ; which is defcribed in the fixteenth chapter, verfe feventeenth, &c.

And the fame event is again reprefented in the latter part of the nineteenth chapter, and in the beginning of the twentieth. " And I faw heaven opened, and behold, a white horfe : And he that fat upon him was called faithful and true, and in righteoufnefs he doth judge and make war." From the following defcription it appears, that this perfon is Jefus Chrift prepared, and going forth to deftroy his enemies on earth. And an angel is feen ftanding in the fun, in the moft confpicuous place, calling with a loud voice upon all the fowls of the air to come "to the fupper of the great God,"

to

to eat the flefh of kings and captains, &c. and the flefh of *all men,* both free and bond, both fmall and great. And he faw the beaft and the kings of the earth, and their armies *gathered together,* to make war againft him that fat on the horfe, and againft his army." And the beaft and falfe prophet were deftroyed by him ; and the remnant of thofe who joined with the beaft and were enemies to Chrift, were flain by him. This battle, and the deftruction of the enemies of Chrift, does not follow in time, and is not to take place after the events mentioned in the firft part of this chapter, viz. the joy and praife in heaven, upon the reigning of Chrift on earth, and the bride, the Lamb's wife, making herfelf ready, &c. but is a repeated and more particular reprefentation of what is to precede that happy event, which had been before mentioned in the fixteenth chapter, from the thirteenth verfe to the end of it. There the kings of the earth, and the whole world, are faid to be *gathered together to battle* ; " The battle of the great day of God Almighty." So here " The beaft and the kings of the earth, and their armies, are *gathered together to make war* againft him that fat on the horfe." And there the battle is defcribed as coming on, upon the pouring out of the feventh vial, and great Babylon, which is the fame with the beaft, and the falfe prophet, and all the enemies of Chrift, are deftroyed in battle. Which is exactly parallel with the war and battle of which there is a more particular defcription in the nineteenth chapter, and muft be one and the fame event. This is confirmed, by what immediately follows this deftruction of the enemies of Chrift, in the beginning of the twentieth chapter, which, as has been obferved, is the fame event with that defcribed in the nineteenth chapter by the marriage of the Lamb, whofe bride, that is the church, was made ready, and arrayed in fine linen, clean and white. A more particular and remarkable defcription of this fame thing, in the twentieth chapter, is in the following words.

" And I faw an angel come down from heaven, having the key of the bottomlefs pit, and a great chain in his hand. And he laid hold on the dragon, that old ferpent, which is the devil and fatan, and bound him a thoufand years, and caft him into the bottomlefs pit, and fhut him up, and fet a feal upon him, that he fhould deceive the nations no more, till the thoufand years fhould be fulfilled : And after that, he muft be loofed a little feafon. And I faw thrones, and they fat upon them, and judgment was given unto them. And I faw the fouls of them that were beheaded for the witnefs of Jefus, and for the word of God, and which had not worfhipped the beaft, neither his image, neither had received his mark upon their foreheads, or in their hands : And they lived and reigned with Chrift a thoufand years. But the reft of the dead lived not again until the thoufand years were finifhed. This is the firft refurrection. Bleffed and holy is he that hath part in the firft refurrection. On fuch the fecond death hath no power ; but they fhall be priefts of God, and of Chrift, and fhall reign with him a thoufand years."

A particular explanation of this paffage of fcripture will be attempted in the next fection. That it does exprefs and confirm the truth which is contained in the numerous prophecies which have been mentioned, and which is fet up to be proved in this fection, the following obfervations will fhow.

1. This event here predicted, is to take place after the overthrow of the Roman antichriftian kingdom, and the deftruction of all the enemies of Chrift and his church on earth. This is evident from the account of the deftruction of thefe in the prophecy immediately preceding thefe words, and upon which the glorious fcene opened in this paffage, is to take place. And the fame is predicted in the laft part of the fixteenth chapter, as has been fhown. This is agreeable to the prophecies of the fame event, in the Pfalms, and by Daniel, and others, viz. that the time of the reign of Chrift, and of the faints on earth, fhall fucceed the deftruction of the wicked, and the total overthrow of all the preceding kingdoms and powers in the world, which has been from time to time obferved upon them, when they were tranfcribed. And in this very paffage, fatan himfelf is reprefented as bound, and caft out of the earth, and fhut up in the bottomlefs pit, antecedent to the reign of Chrift, and his followers, in the world ; which neceffarily implies the total ruin of his caufe and kingdom on earth, and the extirpation of all the wicked, who are his children and fervants. Therefore, the time here predicted, is not yet come.

2. All this is to take place before the end of the world, and the day of judgment. This is very evident and certain, fince it is faid, that when this happy time of a thoufand years is ended, fatan fhall be loofed out of his prifon, and fhall go out to deceive the nations which are in the four quarters of the earth : And then, after this, Chrift is reprefented as coming to judgment, of which

E                                    there

there is a particular account ; and of the final and eternal deſtruction of all his enemies.

3. Chriſt is here ſaid to reign, and his ſaints to reign with him,
which, without any doubt, is the ſame event, and the ſame period,
which is foretold by Daniel and other Prophets, as a moſt happy
and joyful time, when that nation and thoſe men who will **not**
ſerve Jeſus Chriſt, ſhall be deſtroyed ; and there ſhall be given to
him dominion and glory, and a kingdom, that all people, nations,
and languages fhould ſerve him. And the kingdom and dominion, and the greatneſs of the kingdom under the whole heaven,
ſhall be given to the ſaints of the Moſt High, and all dominions
ſhall ſerve him. And the extent and univerſality of the kingdom
of Chriſt, and of thoſe who reign with him, as including all nations and all men, is ſuppoſed and implied in his binding ſatan
and caſting him out, " that he ſhould *deceive the nations no more,*
till the thouſand years fhould be fulfilled." Satan is ſaid to deceive the whole world.\* And when he is caſt out of the whole
world, Jeſus Chriſt and his people will take poſſeſſion of it, and
reign in all the earth.

4. Chriſt and his people are to reign on earth A THOUSAND
YEARS.† All have not been agreed in the length of time denoted
here by a thouſand years. Some have ſuppoſed that a thouſand
years, is uſed indefinitely, not to expreſs any preciſe number of
years, but a great number of years, or a long time. But this cannot reaſonably be admitted as the ſenſe of the expreſſion here, ſince
this preciſe number of years, is mentioned ſix times in this paſſage,
which appears inconſiſtent with its being uſed in ſuch an indefinite,
vague ſenſe. And beſides, there is nothing in the connection here,
or in the nature or circumſtances of the caſe, to lead any one to
underſtand this number, as put indefinitely.

There are others who ſuppoſe, that theſe are to be underſtood
to be a thouſand prophetical years, that is, as many years as there
are days in a thouſand literal years, a day being put for a year.—
According to this way of reckoning, a thouſand years are put for
three hundred and ſixty thouſand years ; for in that age, a year
was reckoned to conſiſt of three hundred and ſixty days. It is
ſaid, that in this book of Revelation, a day is conſtantly put for a
year. A thouſand, two hundred and ſixty days, mean ſo many
years,

---

\* Chap. xii. 9.      † Hence this time is called the MILLENNIUM, which
ſignifies a thouſand years.

years, and forty two months, mean as many years, as there are
days in fo many months, reckoning thirty days to each month, as
they then did ; which therefore amount to the fame number of
years, i. e. one thoufand, two hundred and fixty years.  And a
time and times, and half a time, i. e. three years and an half,
mean as many years as there are days in three years and an half ;
which are juft as many as there are in forty two months ; that is,
one thoufand, two hundred and fixty years.  It is therefore concluded, that thefe thoufand years, muft be underftood in the fame
way ; that is, that a day is put for a year ; which will amount to
three hundred and fixty thoufand years.

It is acknowledged that this fuppofition is fupported by fome
colour of argument, and plaufibility :  But there are objections
to it, fome of which will be mentioned.

1. It does by no means follow that thefe are prophetical years,
in the fenfe mentioned, becaufe a day is put for a year, in other
places in this prophecy.  There may be reafons for putting a day
for a year, in other inftances ; and yet there be no reafon for putting a thoufand years for as many years as there are days in a
thoufand years, in this inftance ; and therefore no reafon for underftanding them fo.  And a day is not put for a year in every
other inftance in this book.  The dead bodies of the two witnefles
are faid to lie in the ftreet of the city, three days and an half,*
which do not mean three years and an half, as no event refpecting
them can be made confiftent with fuch a meaning.

2. The number, *a thoufand years*, being repeated fo many times
in one fhort paragraph, feems to be a reafon that it is to be underftood literally, for juft fo many years, and not fo many prophetical
years.  Efperially, as there is nothing in this cafe to lead us to
underftand it in the latter fenfe ; but it may, as confiftently with
every thing in this book, and this prophecy in particular, and more
fo, as will be now obferved, be underftood literally.  And it is
farther to be obferved, that there is no inftance in this book, or in
the whole Bible, where a precife number is fo often repeated in
the fame words, that is not to be underftood literally.

3. It feems to be out of all proper proportion, to fuppofe there
will be fo long a time as three hundred and fixty thoufand years
of profperity and happinefs, and of great and univerfal holinefs in
this world, the habitation of an apoftate, finful race of men ; and

E 2 but

* Chap. xi. 11.

but fix thoufand years of evil times.   And this does not appear
confiftent with this world being reprefented as an *evil world*, as it
is in the fcripture: Or with its being curfed in confequence of
man's rebellion.   One thoufand years may be an exception out
of feven thoufand, in which the curfe may be mitigated, and in a
great meafure removed; and yet, on the whole, or the whole
taken together, it may be confidered and called, an evil and áccurfed
world, for man's fake.   But if there were to be only fix thoufand
years of evil and the curfe, and three hundred and fixty thoufand
years of good and a blefling, it would not, on the whole, be an evil
or curfed, but a happy and blefled world.

4.  It has been obferved, that the natural world is evidently a
defigned type or fhadow of the moral world, efpecially of the redemption by Chrift.   And that creating it in fix days, and then
refting on the feventh, is defigned to be a type of bringing the
moral world in the work of redemption, to a flate of reft ; that
there are to be fix thoufand years in which every thing with refpect to redemption and the kingdom of Chrift, is to be done and
prepared, for a feventh thoufand years of peace and reft, and joy
in this glorious work.   And it will be fhown in the fequel, that
there are inftitutions in the Mofaic ritual, which point out the fame
thing.   The Apoftle Peter feems to allude to this, when fpeaking
of thecoming of Chrift, and the end of the world.   " But beloved,
be not ignorant of this one thing, that one day is with the Lord
as a thoufand years, and a thoufand years as one day.   The Lord
is not flack concerning his promife ; but the day of the Lord will
come as a thief in the night," &c.*   Hence the conftant revolution of weeks, confifting of feven days, is an emblem of the revolution of time, which will come to an end, when the world has
exifted feven thoufand years.   And there has been a tradition
among both Jews and Chriftians, agreeable to this fentiment.†—
                                                             Now,

* 2 Peter iii. 8, 9, 10.

† " There is an old tradition both among Jews and Chriftians, that at the
end of fix thoufand years, the Meffiah fhall come, and the world fhall be renewed,
the reign of the wicked one fhall ceafe, and the reign of the faints upon earth
fhall begin." Newton's Differtations on the Prophecies. Vol. I. Page 490.—
And again, Vol. III. Page 410.—" According to tradition, thefe thoufand years
of the reign of Chrift and the faints, will be the feventh millennary of the
world ; for as God created the world in fix days, and refted on the feventh, fo
the world, it is argued, will continue fix thoufand years, and the feventh thou-
                                                             fand

Now, this fentiment and tradition fuppofe, that the thoufand years of the Millennium, is but one literal thoufand years, or the feventh part of the time in which the world is to ftand. And as far as there is any weight in them, oppofe and overthrow the notion that the world will not come to an end, till it has exifted three hundred and fixty thoufand years, after the Millennium fhall begin.

5. All the ends of fuch a day of peace and profperity, of victory, triumph and falvation to the church on earth, and of the fo much celebrated reign of Chrift with his faints, in this world, will be fully anfwered in a literal thoufand years, fo far as it can be learned what they are, from fcripture ; or man can conceive them to be ; as much and as fully anfwered, as they could be in hundreds of thou- fands of years, or in any fuppofed length of time.

Satan will be as much defeated, and his kingdom and intereft wholly deftroyed in the world ; the caufe of wickednefs, and evil men, will be entirely ruined and loft, and they all banifhed from the earth. The wifdom, power, grace, truth and faithfulnefs of Chrift will have a proper and glorious manifeftation, by intro- ducing fuch a ftate, and continuing it as long as is moft for his glory, and the beft good of his church, though it fhall continue but a thoufand years. The church may have all the reward and enjoyment in that time, that it is proper or defirable that it fhould have on earth ; and it may be wifeft and beft, then to take it to a more perfect, happy and glorious ftate in heaven. A thoufand years will be time enough for Chrift to fhow what he can do, in bringing good out of evil, and vindicating his caufe and church, and triumphing glorioufly over all oppofition from earth and hell, and filling the world with his powerful prefence and kingdom, with the knowledge of the glory of the Lord ; with holinefs and happinefs. There will be full opportunity in this time, to fhow and demonftrate, from fact and abundant experience, what is the nature, beauty and excellence of chriftianity ; that it is exactly fuited to form the world into a ftate of love, union and happinefs ; and that all the preceding evils among mankind have been chiefly owing to ignorance or neglect of Chrift, and the true fpirit of chriftianity, and oppofition to thofe in life or heart, or both. And this will be time enough to fhow, that all means are ineffectual to

reclaim

fand will be the great *fabbatifm*, or holy reft, to the people of God : *One day being with the Lord as a thoufand years, and a thoufand years as one day."*— 2 Peter iii. 8.

reclaim man from fin; and that this can be effected by nothing but the fpirit of God, poured down in plentiful effufions ; and to give a fample and foretafte of the beauty, happinefs and glory of the holy fociety and redeemed church in heaven.

And in this thoufand years the work of redemption, and falvation, may be fully accomplifhed, in the utmoft extent and glory of it. In this time, in which the world will be foon filled with real chriftians, and continue full, by conftant propagation, to fupply the place of thofe who will leave the world ; there will be many thoufands born and live on earth, to each one that had been born and lived in the preceding fix thoufand years. So that if they who fhall be born in that thoufand years, fhall be all, or moft of them, faved, as they will be, there will, on the whole, be many thoufands of mankind faved, to one that fhall be loft.*

The only end that can be imagined would be anfwered by protracting this time of the profperity of the church in this world, is, that greater numbers of mankind might exift, and be faved. But that this is really defirable or beft, all things confidered, there is not the leaft evidence. A defire that more of mankind fhould be faved than will be faved, in a thoufand years of the prevalence of holinefs and falvation, in all the families of the earth, never could be fatisfied : For though three hundred and fixty thoufand years fhould be added, and all fhould be faved who lived in that time; ftill, for the fame reafon that this is defired, it will be equally defirable, and more fo, that the time of falvation fhould be lengthened out yet longer ; and fo on without end. This reafon for making the time longer, that more may be faved, cannot ceafe ; and a defire of more time, on this ground, or for this reafon, is like the four things which Solomon mentions as never fatisfied, and fay not it is enough. It is moft wife and beft, that a certain number and proportion of mankind fhould be faved : And God only knows what this number is, how great, and what proportion it bears to the whole human race. And no man has any reafon to think, that this number will not be compleated within a literal thoufand years, after the Millennium commences. Nor can there be the leaft evidence from any quarter, that it will not, unlefs there be evidence that the Millennium contains a longer time; which is the queftion under confideration. And it is fuppofed that

* See Bellamy's Sermon on the Millennium.

that no evidence of this has yet been produced, or can be at prefent: And it is certain, that the falvation of more of mankind,
were the time to be longer, is no reafon why it fhould be longer.
But this will be beft, and moft infallibly decided by the event which
will take place in due feafon : Which perhaps cannot be determined with certainty now, or fo that all fhall be fatisfied and a-
greed in the matter.  And it may not be wife to be very confi-
dent on either fide of the queftion.

THE evidence has now been produced from fcripture, that
there is a time coming, in which the caufe of Chrift fhall prevail
in this world ; and his kingdom fpread and fill the earth, as it has
never yet done ; in which time, the church and people of Chrift
fhall come to a ftate of peace and profperity ; when the kingdom
of fatan fhall be utterly deftroyed ; and all wicked men fhall be put
down, and caft out of the earth, and there fhall be none to deftroy,
hurt or oppofe the truth and ways of Chrift, or his people : And
this happy, glorious day fhall laft a thoufand years.

This is foretold, not by one fingle prophecy, but is repeatedly
and abundantly mentiond in the facred, prophetic writings, and
reprefented by a variety of ftrong expreffions, and by different
fimilitudes, and in figurative language : And yet all perfectly a-
gree to point out the fame thing.  And there are many prophecies of the fame event, by Ifaiah, and in other parts of the Bible,
which have not been particularly mentioned.

Nothing has yet taken place in favour of the church of Chrift,
and in oppofition to his enemies, which is in any meafure anfwerable to thefe predictions.  By far the greater part of mankind
have been in a ftate of ignorance of chriftianity, or of oppofition
to it, ever fince the gofpel has been preached to men ; and fatan
has had a greater and ftronger kingdom on earth, than Chrift,
moft of the time fince his afcenfion.  And fin, and real oppofition
to Chrift, in principle and practice, have abounded in every age,
even among nominal chriftians.  The overthrow of the Jews by
the Romans, and the confequent fpread of chriftianity among the
Gentiles, were events favourable to the church of Chrift, and
were a pledge and type of what he will yet do, in overthrowing his
enemies and delivering his church, in the latter days.  And fo
was the overthrow of heathen Rome, and the fpread and prevalence of chriftianity through all the Roman empire, in the days

of

of the Emperor Conſtantine, in the fourth century. But this was of ſhort continuance, and within twenty years the church fell into a ſtate of great calamity, by diviſiqns, contentions, and hereſies ; and the empire was involved in confuſion and war. And from that time to this, the church has been in a low, afflicted ſtate. The many promiſes made to Iſrael by the prophets, of reſtoration to a long abiding ſtate of obedience, holineſs and proſperity, have not been in any meaſure fulfilled to that nation, nor to the church, including Jews and Gentiles, repreſented and typified by Iſrael, Jeruſalem, Mount Zion, &c. If ſuch a day of proſperity of the church of Chriſt, comprehending Jews and Gentiles, and all nations, were not yet to come, great part of the prophecies in the Bible could have but a very low and little meaning, and would be in a great meaſure, if not wholly, uſeleſs. Whereas, if they be underſtood according to the moſt natural, plain import of them, they open a moſt pleaſing, wonderful ſcene, ſuited to ſupport and animate the chriſtian, and fill him with gratitude and joy, on the agreeable proſpect.

It appears reaſonable and deſirable, that Jeſus Chriſt, who ſuffered ſhame and reproach in this world, and was condemned and put to death as a malefactor, by men, ſhould have this reproach wiped off in the ſight of all men, and that the cauſe in which he ſuffered and died, ſhould prevail and be victorious in this ſame world, where he ſuffered and died: That he ſhould, agreeably to ancient prophecies, be here on earth, " Exalted, and extolled, and be very high. As many were aſtoniſhed at him (his viſage was ſo marred more than any man, and his form more than the ſons of men) ſo ſhall he ſprinkle many nations, and kings ſhall ſhut their mouths at him: For that which had not been told them ſhall they ſee ; and that which they had not heard, ſhall they conſider. He ſhall ſee of the travail of his ſoul, and ſhall be ſatisfied. He ſhall divide the ſpoil with the ſtrong; becauſe he hath poured out his ſoul unto death ; and was numbered with the tranſgreſſors."*

And it appears very deſirable, that the enemies of Chriſt and his church, ſhould meet with diſappointment, be defeated and confounded in this world, and that the reproach which has been caſt upon the church ſhould be removed : That the church ſhould put on her beautiful garments, and ſhine in the true beauties of chriſtianity :

* Iſai. lii. 13, 14, 15. liii. 11, 12.

chriftianity: That it fhould be feen from experiment in this world, what chriftianity is, when acted out, according to the true nature and fpirit of it ; and that this, and this only, can render men and fociety happy in this ftate. All this is therefore predict- ed, and promifed. " Behold, at that time I will undo all that afflict thee, and I will fave her that halteth, and gather her that was driven out, and I will get them praife and fame in every land, where they have been put to fhame : For I will make you a name and a praife among all people of the earth."*

One reafon why this day of falvation is delayed fo long after the death and refurrection of Chrift, doubtlefs is, that there may be proper and full opportunity to difcover the depravity and wicked- nefs of man, and the infufficiency of all means that can be ufed, or methods taken, to bring men to repentance, and a cordial fub- miffion to Chrift, unlefs accompanied by the fpecial, omnipotent influences of the Holy Spirit, to renew their hearts : And clearly to manifeft the natural enmity in the hearts of mankind againft Chrift, and the truths of the gofpel, and their ftrong difpofition, and unconquerable by all poffible external means and advantages, to oppofe, and pervert the gofpel, and abufe it to the worft pur- pofes ; that it may appear in the moft clear and ftriking light, how greatly and wholly depraved, and utterly loft, men are, unlefs they be faved by the wafhing of regeneration, and the renewing of the Holy Ghoft ; and that the whole praife and glory of the falvation of every one, may be afcribed to the fovereign grace of Chrift, and man be forever abafed. When God has fufficiently tried men, and ufed a variety of the moft proper and powerful means to bring the world to repentance, and all has proved in vain, he will then pour out his fpirit upon all, and renew their hearts, and converts will fpring up as grafs after fhowers of rain ; and the obftinacy of man, and the power and fovereign grace of Chrift, will be ac- knowledged by all ; and that men are faved, not by human might or power, but by the fpirit of the Lord.†

And it appears proper and wife, that this day of profperity and falvation, fhould be in the latter end of the world, in the laft times, as this is fuited to excite and fupport the faith and patience of chriftians, who live in the preceding dark and evil times ; and to encourage and animate them to faithfulnefs and conftaney, in fol- lowing Chrift, and adherence to his caufe, in the midft of tempta-

F                                                                                            tions

tions and trials; and this use is made of it in the scripture, especially in the book of Revelation.   And this is suited to excite the prayers of christians in all the preceding ages of darkness, affliction and suffering, and the prevalence of sin, and satan, for the coming and kingdom of Christ ; which he has prescribed as the first and most important petition in the pattern of prayer which he has given.   " Our Father, who art in heaven, hallowed be thy name. *Thy kingdom come.* Thy will be done in earth as it is in heaven."   Daniel was excited and encouraged to fast and pray for the deliverance of the people of God, from their affliction and distress in their captivity, by finding that this was foretold and promised by Jeremiah the Prophet.*   And this has actually excited christians to pray for this event, in all ages of the church ; and doubtless they will be awakened and stirred up to pray more generally, constantly, and fervently for this important, glorious event, as the approach of it is found by prophecy to be nearer : And it will be introduced in answer to the prayers of thousands and millions, who have been, and who will yet be, crying to God night and day ; resolving not to keep silence, or give him any rest, till he establish, and till he make Jerusalem a praise in the earth.†   For he will be enquired of for this by his church and people, to do it for them."‡

        * Dan. ix. 2, 3, 4.    † Isai. lxii. 6, 7.    ‡ Ezek. xxxvi. 37.

# SECTION II.

*In which it is considered, in what the Millennium will consist, and what will be the peculiar happiness and glory of that day, according to Scripture.*

THERE have been, and still are, very different opinions, respecting the Millennium, and the events which will take place in that day ; which are grounded chiefly on the six first verses in the twentieth chapter of the Revelation, which passage has been brought into view, in the preceding section ; but is to be more particicularly considered in this.                        Some

Some have fuppofed, that this paffage is to be taken literally, as importing that at that time, Jefus Chrift will come in his human nature, from heaven to earth ; and fet his kingdom up here, and reign vifibly, and perfonally, and with diftinguifhed glory on earth. And that the bodies of the martyrs, and other eminent chriftians, will then be raifed from the dead, in which they fhall live and reign with Chrift here on earth, a thoufand years. And fome fuppofe, that all the faints, the true friends to God and Chrift, who have lived before that time, will then be raifed from the dead, and live on earth perfectly holy, during this thoufand years. And this they fuppofe, is meant by the firft refurrection. Thofe who agree in general in this notion of the Millennium, differ with refpect to many circumftances, which it is needlefs to mention here.

Others have underftood this paragraph of fcripture, in a figurative fenfe. That by this reign of Chrift on earth, is not meant his coming from heaven to earth, in his human, vifible nature ; but his taking to himfelf his power, and utterly overthrowing the kingdom of fatan, and fetting up his own kingdom in all the world, which before this had been confined to very narrow bounds ; and fubduing all hearts to a willing fubjection, and thus reigning over all men, who fhall then be in the world, and live in that thoufand years. And by " The fouls of them which were beheaded for the witnefs of Jefus, and for the word of God, and which had not worfhipped the beaft, neither his image, neither had received his mark upon their foreheads, or in their hands," living again and reigning with Chrift a thoufand years ; they fuppofe, is not meant a literal refurrection, or the refurrection of their bodies, which is not afferted here, as there is nothing faid of their bodies, or of their being raifed to life : But that they fhall live again and reign with Chrift, in the revival, profperity, reign and triumph of that caufe and intereft in which they lived, and for the promotion of which they died ; and in whofe death, the caufe feemed in a meafure, and for a time, to die and be loft. And they fhall live again in their fucceffors, who fhall arife and ftand up with the fame fpirit, and in the fame caufe, in which they lived and died, and fill the world and reign with Chrift a thoufand years, agreeable to ancient prophecies. " The meek fhall inherit the earth. And the kingdom and dominion, and the greatnefs of the kingdom under the whole heaven, fhall be given to the people of the faints of the Moft High ; whofe kingdom is an everlafting kingdom,

and

and all dominions fhall ferve him." And they fuppofe, that this revival of the truths and caufe of Chrift, by the numerous inhabitants of the earth, rifing up to a new and holy life, and filling the world with holinefs and happinefs, is that which is here called the *firft refurrection,* in diftinction from the fecond, which will confift in the refurrection of the body ; whereas this is a fpiritual refurrection ; a refurrection of the truths and caufe of Chrift, which had been in a great degree, dead and loft ; and a refurrection of the fouls of men, by the renovation of the Holy Ghoft.

That this important paffage of fcripture, is to be underftood in the figurative fenfe, laft mentioned, is very probable, if not certain. And the following confiderations are thought fufficient to fupport it.

1. Moft, if not all the prophecies in this book, are delivered in figurative language, referring to types and events recorded in the Old Teftament ; and in imitation of the language of the ancient Prophets. And this was proper and even neceffary in the beft manner to anfwer the ends of prophecy, as might eafily be fhown, were it neceffary. The firft part of this paffage, all muft allow, is figurative. Satan cannot be bound with a literal, material chain. The key, the great chain, and the feal, cannot be underftood literally. The whole is a figure, and can mean no more than that when the time of the Millennium arrives, or rather previous to it, Jefus Chrift will lay effectual reftraints on fatan, fo that his powerful and prevailing influence by which he has before deceived and deftroyed a great part of mankind, fhall be wholly taken from him, for a thoufand years. And it is moft natural to underftand the other part of the defcription of this remarkable event to be reprefented in the fame figurative language ; as the whole is a reprefentation of one fcene ; efpecially, fince no reafon can be given why it fhould not be underftood fo : And there are reafons againft taking it in a literal fenfe, which will be mentioned in the following particulars.

2. To fuppofe that Chrift fhall come in his human nature to this earth, and live here in his whole perfon vifibly a thoufand years, before the day of judgment, appears to be contrary to feveral paffages of fcripture.

The coming of Chrift, and his appearing at the day of judgment in his human nature, is faid to be his *fecond* appearance, anfwering to his *firft* appearance in his human nature on earth,

from

from his birth to his afcenfion into heaven, which was paft.
" And as it is appointed unto men once to die, but after this the
judgment : So Chrift was once offered to bear the fins of many;
and unto them who look for him fhall he appear the *fecond time*,
without fin, unto falvation."* The appearance here fpoken of,
is the appearance of Chrift at the day of judgment, to complete the
falvation of his church. This could not be his appearing the fecond time, were he thus to appear, and to be bodily prefent in his
human nature on earth, in the time of the Millennium, which is
to take place before the day of judgment. The coming of Chrift,
does not always intend his coming vifibly in his human nature;
but he is faid to come, when he deftroyed the temple and nation
of the Jews, and appeared in favour of his church. So his deftruction of heathen Rome, and delivering his church from that
perfecuting power, was an inftance of his coming. And he will,
in the fame way, come to deftroy antichrift, and the kingdom of
fatan in the world, and introduce the Millennium ; and in thefe
inftances, and others, he may be faid to appear. But his coming
to judgment, and appearing to complete the final deftruction of
all his enemies, and to perfect the falvation of his church, is his
laft coming and appearance. And though this will not be his fecond appearance and coming, in the fenfe now mentioned, and
with reference to thofe inftances of his coming ; yet, as he will
then come and appear vifibly in his human nature ; this will be
his fecond coming and appearance in this way and manner, having
never appeared on earth in his human nature more than once before, or fince his firft afcenfion to heaven, after his incarnation.
Therefore, when the final judgment fhall take place, Chrift is reprefented as being revealed, and coming from heaven, and this is
often called, by way of eminence, his *appearing*; meaning his appearing and coming from heaven in vifible fplendor and glory, in
his whole perfon, in both natures, divine and human. But if he
were here on earth, vifible in his human nature, and reigning in
his glorified body, during the Millennium ; he would be already
here to attend the laft judgment, and he could not be properly
faid to come from heaven, and to be revealed from heaven, becaufe this was done a thoufand years before. Therefore, that
Chrift fhould come from heaven, and appear and reign in his human nature and prefence before the day of judgment, feems to be
contrary to the following fcriptures : " For the Lord himfelf
fhall

* Heb. ix. 27, 28.

fhall *defcend from heaven* with a fhout, with the voice of the arch-
angel, and with the trump of God : And the dead in Chrift fhall
rife firft.   When the Lord Jefus fhall be *revealed from heaven,* with
his mighty angels, in flaming fire, taking vengeance on them that
know not God, &c.   When he *fhall come* to be glorified in his
faints."*   This is evidently his appearing the fecond time, for the
falvation of all them that look for him ;  and were he on earth before this, in the human nature, during the time of the Millennium, how could he be faid to be *revealed,* to *defcend* and *come from*
heaven to judge the world ?

3.  As it feems to be contrary to the above mentioned fcriptures to fuppofe, that Chrift will appear on earth, and reign a
thoufand years ih his human nature ;  fo it appears contrary to all
reafon.   Jefus Chrift is now on the throne of the univerfe, having
all power in heaven and earth given to him as God-man, and
Redeemer, being made head over all things to the church.   He
is in the moft proper, agreeable, and convenient fituation to govern the world, and take care of his church.   It does not appear
agreeable to his ftation and office, as king and head over all things,
for him to defcend in the human nature, and erect a throne on
earth ;  which, fo far as can be conceived, would be no advantage
to his perfon, defign and work ;  but very much to the contrary.
He is gone to heaven in the human nature, that he might reign
there, till his enemies are made his footftool, and all things fhall
be fubdued under him.   And his church on earth will enjoy him
to as great a degree, and as much advantage, as if he were perfonally on earth in the human nature, and more ;  and will have as
great enjoyment of his prefence.   He is now in the beft fituation
to be adored and worfhipped by his church on earth.   Though
they now do not fee him,  yet believing and loving him, they rejoice with joy unfpeakable and full of glory.   And it would not tend
to increafe this faith, love and joy, to have him come from heaven,
and live in fome place on earth, in his human nature ;  but the
contrary :  For but few, compared with the whole inhabitants of
the world, could have accefs to him, or fee him more than they
now do.   And when the human nature is in heaven, all may
equally have accefs to him, love and worfhip him.   His church
and kingdom on earth will be as happy, fplendid and glorious, as
if he were on earth, as he is now in heaven, and much more fo ;
for thefe will confift in his fpiritual prefence and influence, which

may

* 1 Theff. iv, 16.   2 Theff. i.  7, 8, 10.

may be as great while his human nature is in heaven, as if it were on earth ; and in their holy conformity to Chrift, which would not be increafed by his being in that fenfe on earth. It hence appears in no refpect advantageous or defirable, but the contrary, that Jefus Chrift fhould come perfonally in the human nature from heaven to earth, to reign here with his church, or that he fhould thus appear, till he fhall come to judgment. It is therefore unreafonable to expect or fuppofe he will thus come, unlefs it were exprefsly afferted in fcripture, which it certainly is not ; but there are fome, if not many paffages, which feem to be inconfiftent with it.

It may be proper to obferve here, that the queftion refpecting the manner in which Chrift will reign on earth in the Millennium, has no concern with the queftion concerning the literal or figurative meaning of this paffage, as the former does not depend upon the latter : For no man will fuppofe, that Chrift's reigning on earth, is to be underftood in a figurative fenfe. If he fhall reign on earth in the hearts of men, by their voluntary fubjection to him, he will reign as literally, as if he were prefent on earth in his humanity. The queftion, whether this paffage is to be underftood literally or figuratively, refpects the fouls of them that were beheaded for the witnefs of Jefus, &c. their living and reigning with Chrift a thoufand years. This therefore leads to other obfervations.

4. The Apoftle Paul in his writings, does not appear to expect to have his body raifed from the dead to live here on earth again, after he died ; or fay any thing to lead the chriftians of this day to expect any fuch thing, but the contrary.

He fays, " It is appointed unto man once to die, but after this the judgment." And leads chriftians to look forward to the fecond coming of Chrift, when he will come to judgment, as the next great event that will immediately refpect them ; which feems to be inconfiftent with the faints having their bodies raifed, and living in this world again, a thoufand years before the day of judgment. He addreffes chriftians in the following words, " If ye then be rifen with Chrift, feek thofe things which are above, where Chrift fitteth on the right hand of God. Set your affection on things above, not on things on earth. For ye are dead, and your life is hid with Chrift in God. When Chrift, who is

our

our life, fhall appear, then fhall ye alfo appear with him in glory."* He directs them to expect and feek enjoyment in heaven where Chrift is ; and not to expect that he will leave his throne there, till he fhall appear the fecond time, to receive his faints to glory in heaven. For appearing with Chrift in glory, means, appearing with him in heaven, as that is the place of glory, where the redeemed are brought to be glorified, to be where Chrift is, to behold his glory. The Apoftle Peter, fpeaking of the diffolution of the heavens and earth, fays, " Neverthelefs we, according to his promife, look for new heavens and a new earth, wherein dwelleth righteoufnefs."† Some have fuppofed, that this is the Millennium ftate, which fhall take place after the general conflagration, by which the earth will be renewed; in which a perfectly holy and happy ftate fhall commence, to which all the faints who had died fhall be raifed, &c. But fuch a notion cannot be reconciled to other paffages of fcripture, in which, as has been obferved, the Millennium is reprefented as taking place before the general conflagration and the day of judgment. And after thefe are over, and the wicked are caft into endlefs punifhment,‡ the Apoftle John fays, " And I fay a new heaven and a new earth : For the firft heaven and the firft earth were paffed away ; and there was no more fea."§ By which the heavenly ftate is chiefly if not wholly meant, where redemption and the church wil be perfected. By the new heaven and new earth, is meant the work of redemption, or the church redeemed by Chrift. This is the new creation, infinitely fuperiour to the old creation, the natural world, and more important, excellent and durable ; of which the latter is a faint type or fhadow.

The renovation of the hearts of men, by the Spirit of God, by which they become true chriftians, is in fcripture called a new creature, or as the original words κυνη κτίσις may as well be rendered, *a new creation.* "Therefore, if any man be in Chrift, he is a new creature : Old things are paft away, behold, all things are become new."‖ " For in Chrift Jefus, neither circumcifion availeth any thing, nor uncircumcifion, but a new creature.¶"— Therefore, every true member of the church belongs to the new creation, and is part of it ; and this new creation of the new heaven and new earth, goes on and makes advances, as the church is enlarged

---

* Col. iii. 1, 2, 3, 4.    † 2 Pet. iii. 13.    ‡ Rev. 20.
§ Chap. xxi. 1,    ‖ 2 Cor. v. 17.    ¶ Gal. vi. 15.

larged and rifes to a ftate of greater profperity, and proceeds towards perfection.

The new heavens, and new earth, the redeemed church of Chrift, will be brought to a very happy and glorious ftate in the Millennium, and greater advantages will be made then in this new creation, than were ever made before. Therefore, to this event, the following prophecy of Ifaiah, does chiefly refer, if not wholly. "For behold, I create new heavens, and a new earth. And the former fhall not be remembered, nor come into mind. But be you glad and rejoice forever, in that which I create : For behold, I create Jerufalem a rejoicing, and her people a joy."* It appears from the preceding and following context, that this prophecy refers to the Millennium, in which the new creation, the church of Chrift, will come to the moft perfect and happy ftate to which it will be brought in this world ; from which it will pafs to a perfect ftate, and be completely finifhed, after the general refurrection and judgment. Then the old creation, the heavens and the earth fhall pafs away, and be burnt up, and the new creation fhall be finifhed, and brought to a moft perfect, beautiful, happy and glorious ftate. To the new heaven and new earth, thus completed, wherein that righteoufnefs or true holinefs, which is the beauty, happinefs and glory of the new creation, will *dwell*, i. e. continue and flourifh forever, the Apoftles Peter and John have chief reference in their words, which have been tranfcribed above.

5. It does not appear defirable, or to be any advantage to the departed faints, or to the church of Chrift on earth, to have the bodies of all who have died before the Millennium, raifed from their graves, and come to live a thoufand years in this world, before the general refurrection. They are now perfectly holy and happy ; and fo far as can be conceived, it would be no addition, but a diminution to their happinefs, to come and live in this world, in the body, to eat and drink, and partake of the enjoyments of the world. This would be a degradation, which on no account can be defirable to the fpirits of the juft, now made perfect in heaven. And it would be no advance in the work of redemption, which is then to be carried on in a greater degree, than ever before. Nor would this be any advantage to the church, in that happy ftate, to which it will then be brought ; but the contrary, as they would take up that room in the world, which will be then wanted

G                                                     for

* Chap. lxv. 17, 18.

for thofe who will be born in that day.  And the fpirits of the
juft could not know or enjoy fo much of the profperity and  happinefs of the church, in the falvation of men, were they to  live in
bodies on earth, in that time.  The inhabitants of heaven  have
a more particular and  extenfive knowledge, of what takes place
in favour of the church on earth, than any in this world  have, or
than they could have, were they  to  come and live here.  They
know of every converfion that takes place in this world ; and they
muft have the knowledge of the ftate of the church on earth, and
of every  event  which comes to  pafs  in  favour  of it, and fee  the
whole of its profperity.  And they have great joy  in  every thing
of this kind.  " There is joy in heaven, in prefence  of the angels
of God,  over one finner that repenteth."  How greatly  will the
happinefs and joy in heaven be increafed, when all the inhabitants
of the world fhall be converted to Chrift, and the church of Chrift
fhall fill the earth, and appear in the beauty of holinefs !  Agreeable to this, the inhabitants  of heaven  are reprefented as greatly
rejoicing in the profperity  of the church on earth, and  the overthrow of all her enemies.  " Rejoice over her, thou heaven, and
ye holy Apoftles and Prophets ;  for God hath avenged you on her.
And I heard a great voice of much people in heaven, faying, Hallelujah ;  falvation, and glory, and honour, and power  unto the
Lord our God ;  for he hath judged the great whore, &c.  Let us
be glad and rejoice, and give honour to him ;  for the marriage of
the Lamb is come, and  his wife hath made herfelf ready."*—
Surely none will defire to leave that place of knowledge, light and
joy, and  come and be confined in the body  in this world, which
will be darknefs and folitary, compared with that :  Such a change
of place could be  no privilege or reward ;  but rather a calamity.
Therefore, it is not to be believed, unlefs it be plainly, and in exprefs words revealed ;  which, it is prefumed, it is not.  This leads
to another obfervation.

6.  There is nothing exprefsly faid of the refurrection of the body
in this paffage.  The Apoftle John faw  the *fouls* of them which
were beheaded for the witnefs of Jefus, &c. and they lived and
reigned with Chrift.  The refurrection of the body, is no where
expreffed in fcripture, by the foul's living.  And as there is nothing faid of the body, and he only faw their fouls to live, this does
not appear to be a proper expreffion, to denote the refurrection of
the body, and their living in that.  This therefore does not feem

to

* Rev. xviii. 20.  xix. 1—7.

to be the natural meaning of the words ; and certainly is not the *neceſſary* meaning. We are therefore warranted to look for another meaning, and to acquieſce in it, if one can be found, which is more eaſy and natural, and more agreeable to the whole paſſage, and to the ſcripture in general. Therefore,

7. The moſt eaſy and probable meaning is, that the ſouls of the martyrs, and all the faithful followers of Chriſt, who have lived in the world, and have died before the Millennium ſhall commence, ſhall revive and live again, in their ſucceſſors, who ſhall riſe up in the ſame ſpirit, and in the ſame character, in which they lived and died ; and in the revival and flouriſhing of that cauſe which they eſpouſed, and ſpent their lives in promoting it, which cauſe ſhall appear to be almoſt loſt and dead, previous to the introduction of that glorious day. This is therefore a ſpiritual reſurrection, by which all the inhabitants of the world will be made ſpiritually alive, where ſpiritual death before had reigned ; and they ſhall appear in the ſpirit and power of thoſe martyrs and holy men, who had before lived in the world, and who ſhall live again, in theſe their ſucceſſors, and in the revival of their cauſe, and in the reſurrection of the church, from the very low ſtate, in which it had been before the Millennium, to a ſtate of great proſperity and glory.

This is agreeable to the way of repreſenting things in ſcripture, in other inſtances. John the baptiſt was Elijah, becauſe he roſe in the ſpirit of Elijah, and promoted the ſame cauſe in which Elijah lived and died ; and Elijah revived and lived in John the baptiſt, becauſe he went before Chriſt, in the ſpirit and power of Elijah.* Therefore Chriſt ſays of John, " This is Elijah who was to come."†

It is alſo to be obſerved, that the revival and reſtoration of the church to a ſtate of proſperity, from a dark, low ſtate, is repreſented by a reſurrection to life, or as life from the dead. " Thy dead men ſhall live, together with my dead body ſhall they ariſe ; awake and ſing, ye that dwell in the duſt ; for thy dew is as the dew of herbs, and the earth ſhall caſt out the dead."‡ In the thirty ſeventh chapter of Ezekiel, this is repreſented by bringing dry bones to life ; and from them, raiſing up a very great army.— This is a metaphorical or figurative reſurrection. " Then he ſaid unto me, ſon of man, theſe bones are the whole houſe of Iſrael :

G 2                                   Behold,

* Luke i. 17.      † Matth. xi. 14.      ‡ Iſai. xxvi. 19.

Behold, they fay our bones are dried, and our hope is loft; we are cut off for our parts. Therefore, phephecy and fay unto them, Thus faith the Lord God, Behold, O my people, I will open your graves, and caufe you to come up out of your graves, and bring you into the land of Ifrael." The Apoftle Paul, fpeaking of the converfion of the Jews to Chrift, at the Millennium, fays it fhall be as " life from the dead."*

In the Millennium, there will be a fpiritual refurrection, a refurrection of the fouls of the whole church on earth, and in heaven. All nations will be converted, and the world will be filled with fpiritual life, as it never was before ; and this will be a general refurrection of the fouls of men. This was reprefented in the returning prodigal. The father fays, " This my fon was dead, and is alive." And the Apoftle Paul fpeaks of chriftians as raifed from the dead to life. " But God, who is rich in mercy, for the great love wherewith he loved us, even when we were dead in fins, hath quickened us together with Chrift."† "If ye then be *rifen* with Chrift."‡ And this will be a moft remarkable refurrection of the church on earth from a low, dark, afflicted ftate, to a ftate of great life and joy. It will be multiplied to an exceeding great army, which will cover the face of the earth. And heaven will in a fenfe and degree, come down to earth ; the fpirit of the martyrs, and of all the juft made perfect, will now revive and appear on earth, in their numerous fucceffors, and the joy of thofe in heaven will be greatly increafed.

This is the firft refurrection, in which all they who have a part are bleffed and holy. " Bleffed and holy is he who hath part in the firft refurrection : On fuch the fecond death hath no power." It is implied that *they only* are bleffed and holy, who fhare in this refurrection ; and therefore that all the redeemed in heaven and earth, who are bleffed and holy, are the fubjects of it, or have part in it. All who have been or fhall be raifed from death to fpiritual life, have by this, a part in this firft refurrection ; and they, and they only, fhall efcape the fecond death. This is a farther evidence that this firft refurrection is a fpiritual refurrection, a refurrection of the foul ; for if it were a literal refurrection of the body, no one would think it would include all the happy and holy, all that fhall be faved. The fecond refurrection is to be the refurrection of the body, in which all fhall have part, both the holy

and

* Rom, xi, 15, † Eph. ii. 4, 5. ‡ Col. iii, 1.

and the unholy, the bleffed and the miferable; which is to take
place after the firft refurrection is over, and the Millennium is
ended, and after the rife and deftruction of Gog and Magog;
when the day of judgment fhall come on, of which there is an account in the latter part of this chapter. " And I faw the dead,
fmall and great, ftand before God. And the fea gave up the
dead which were in it: And death and hell delivered up the dead
which were in them: And they were judged every man according to their works." " But the reft of the dead lived not again
until the thoufand years were finifhed." The *reft of the dead*, are
all the dead which have no part in the firft refurrection; that is,
are not holy, and partakers of fpiritual life. This includes all the
wicked who fhall have lived, and fhall die before the Millennium,
the laft of which will be flain, and fwept off the earth previous to
the Millennium, and in order to introduce it, of which there is a
reprefentation in the words immediately preceding the paffage under confideration. " And *the reft* were flain with the fword of
him that fat upon the horfe, which fword proceeded out of his
mouth, and all the fowls were filled with their flefh." In our
tranflation, it is *the remnant.* It is the fame word in the original,
Ὁι λοιποι, which is tranflated *the reft*, in the words tranfcribed a-
bove; and the latter feem to have reference to the former. The
reft of the dead, are the wicked dead, in oppofition to the righteous, who lived again in their fucceffors, who take poffeffion of the
earth and reign; and in the revival and profperity of their caufe,
and the kingdom of which they are members. During this thoufand years, the reft of the dead, all the antichriftian party, and the
wicked enemies of Chrift, who lived and died in the caufe of fatan,
do not live again: They will have no fucceffors on earth, who
fhall rife in their fpirit, and efpoufe and promote their caufe; but
this will be wholly run down and loft, till the thoufand years fhall
be ended: And then they fhall live again a fhort time in their
fucceffors, Gog and Magog, who fhall arife in their fpirit and
caufe, and increafe and prevail, while fatan is loofed again for a
little feafon. This is implied in the words, " But the reft of the
dead lived not again, until the thoufand years were finifhed." It
is fuppofed that they will live again then, which muft be during the
time in which fatan fhall be loofed; for the general refurrection of
the bodies will not be till this is ended. Thefe dead will live then,

juft

juft as the fouls of the martyrs, and all the faithful followers of Chrift, who had died, will live in the Millennium.*

That this prophecy refpects all nations, and the whole of mankind who fhall live in the world in that thoufand years, is evident, in that the binding of fatan refpects them all. " That he fhould deceive the nations no more, till the thoufand years fhould be fulfilled." And this anfwers to a prophecy in Ifaiah. " And he will deftroy in this mountain, the face of the covering caft over *all people,* and the vail that is fpread over *all nations.*"† All nations, the world of mankind therefore, who fhall then live on the earth, will have part in the firft refurrection. And this warrants the application of all the prophecies which have been mentioned in the preceding fection, and others of the fame tenor, to this time. And there is good reafon to believe, that this prophecy, in the firft fix verfes of the twentieth chapter of the Revelation, is expreffed in language beft fuited to anfwer the end of it, if it be underftood as it has been now explained. The meaning is as obvious and plain, as is defirable and proper that of prophecy fhould be, when compared with other prophecies. And it is in the beft manner fuited to fupport and comfort the followers of Chrift, who live before that time; and to animate them to faithfulnefs, conftancy and patience, under all their fufferings in this caufe, while the wicked profper and triumph, and fatan reigns in the world, which is one fpecial end of this revelation. Here they are taught, that an end is to come to the afflictions of the church, and to the triumph of all her enemies. That fatan's kingdom on earth fhall come to an end, and the church fhall rife and fpread, and fill the world; that the caufe in which they labour and fuffer fhall be virtuous, and that all who fuffer in this caufe, and who are faithful to Chrift, fhall live to fee this happy, glorious day, and have a large fhare in it, in proportion to the degree and length of their fufferings,

* " It is very agreeable to the defign and connection of this prophecy, to underftand the reft of the dead, who lived not again till the thoufand years were finifhed, of the reft or remnant, viz. of thofe who were flain with the fword of him that fat on the horfe. Thus the dead church raifed to life, and living and reigning for a thoufand years, and the enemies of the church remaining dead, and not living again till the thoufand years were finifhed, will exactly agree in the fame figurative meaning. This will be a fenfe confiftent with the refurrection of the antichriftian party again, for a little feafon, after the thoufand years fhall be finifhed." Mr. Lowman's Note on Rev. xx. 5. † Ifaiah xxv. 7.

ings, labours, and perfevering patience and fidelity, in the caufe of Chrift and his church.

The way is now prepared, to confider and fhow more particularly, in what the happinefs and glory of the Millennium will confift ; and what particular circumftances will attend the church at that day : What is revealed concerning this by exprefs prophecies, and what is implied in them, or may be deduced as confequences from what is exprefsly declared. It will be no wonder if fome miftakes fhould be made on this point; but it is hoped if there fhould be any, they will not be very hurtful : And it is apprehended that the greateft error will be in falling fhort, and not coming up to the reality, in the defcription of the happinefs and glory of that day ; for doubtlefs, our ideas of thefe, when raifed to the higheft of which we are at prefent capable, fall vaftly fhort of the truth. There is good reafon to conclude, however, that the church, and chriftians, will not be perfectly holy in that day ; but that every one will be attended with a degree of finful imperfection, while in the body, however great may be his attainments and advantages in knowledge and holinefs. Doubtlefs the infpired declarations, that " There is no man which finneth not—There is not a juft man upon earth, that doeth good and finneth not—That if any who profeffes to be a chriftian, fay he hath no fin, he deceiveth himfelf, and the truth is not in him," will remain true to the end of the world, even in the Millennium ; and there will be no perfection on this fide heaven. The apoftacy which will take place at the end of the Millennium, can be better accounted for, on the fuppofition that the faints will not be perfect in that time, and feems to fuppofe it. Though they may, and doubtlefs will, have vaftly higher degrees of light and holinefs, than any fhall have before that time ; yet they will be far from being wholly without fin.

It is moft probable, that every individual perfon who fhall then live will be a real chriftian ; and all will doubtlefs be members of the church, in that day. That is the time when " all fhall know the Lord, from the leaft to the greateft." God fays to his church, fpeaking of that day, " Thy people alfo fhall be all righteous."*
" Awake, awake, put on thy ftrength, O Zion, put on thy beautiful garments, O Jerufalem, the holy city : For henceforth there fhall no more come unto thee the uncircumcifed and the unclean."†

The

The following things will take place in the Millennium in an eminent degree, as they never did before ; which may be mentioned as generals, including many particulars, fome of which will be afterwards fuggefted.

I. That will be a time of eminent holinefs, when it fhall be acted out by all, in a high degree, in all the branches of it, fo as to appear in its true beauty, and the happy effects of it. This will be the peculiar glory, and the fource of the happinefs of the Millennium. The Prophet Zechariah, fpeaking of that day, fays, " In that day, fhall there be upon the bells of the horfes, Holiness unto the Lord ; and the pots of the Lord's houfe fhall be like the bowls before the altar. Yea, every pot in Jerufalem and in Judah, fhall be holinefs unto the Lord of hofts."*— In thefe metaphorical expreffions, is declared the eminent degree of holinefs of that day, which will confecrate every thing, even all the utenfils and the common bufinefs and enjoyments of life, unto the Lord.

Holinefs confifts in love to God, and to man, with every affection and exercife implied in this, which being expreffed and acted out, appears in the exercife of piety towards God, in every branch of it ; and of righteoufnefs and goodnefs, or difinterefted benevolence towards man, including ourfelves. This, fo far as it fhall take place, will banifh all the evils which have exifted and prevailed in the world ; and becoming univerfal, and rifing to a high and eminent degree, will introduce a ftate of enjoyment and happinefs, which never was known before on earth ; and render it a refemblance of heaven in a high degree.

This will be effected by the abundant influences of the Holy Spirit, poured down on men more univerfally, and in more conftant and plentiful effufions, than ever before ; for all holinefs in man, is the effect of the Holy Spirit. That day will be, in a peculiar fenfe, *the difpenfation of the Holy Spirit,* when he will appear as the author of all holinefs, by whofe influence alone divine revealed truth, and all religious inftitutions and means, become efficacious and falutary ; by which he will have peculiar honour, in the holinefs and falvation which fhall then take place. The prophecies of fcripture which refpect the Millennium, reprefent it in this light. God, fpeaking by Ifaiah of that time, fays, " I will pour water upon him that is thirfty, and floods upon the dry ground : I will pour my fpirit upon thy feed, and my bleffing upon thine offspring.

* Chap. xiv. 20, 21,

offspring. And they fhall fpring up as among the grafs, as willows by the water courfes." And the fame time and event is mentioned as the effect of the Holy Spirit, poured out upon the church. "Neither will I hide my face any more from them : *For I have poured out my Spirit upon the houfe of Ifrael,* faith the Lord God."* The fame event is predicted by the Prophet Joel. "And it fhall come to pafs afterward, that I will pour out my Spirit upon all flefh. And alfo upon the fervants, and upon the handmaids in thefe days, will I pour out my Spirit."† The Apoftle Peter, applies this paffage in Joel, to the pouring out of the Spirit, on the Apoftles and others on the day of Penticoft.‡ But this prophecy was fulfilled only in a fmall degree then. This was but the beginning, the firft fruits, which will iffue in that which is unfpeakably greater, more extenfive and glorious in the days of the Millennium, to which this prediction has chief refpect, and when it will have the full and moft complete accomplifhment.

II. There will be a great increafe of light and knowledge to a degree vaftly beyond what has been before. This is indeed implied in the great degree of holinefs, which has been mentioned. For knowledge, mental light, and holinefs, are infeparably connected ; and are, in fome refpects, the fame. Holinefs is true light and difcerning, fo far as it depends upon a right tafte, and confifts in it ; and it is a thirft after every kind and degree of ufeful knowledge ; and this defire and thirft for knowledge, will be great and ftrong, in proportion to the degree of holinefs exercifed : And forms the mind to conftant attention, and to make fwift advances in underftanding and knowledge ; and becomes a ftrong guard againft miftakes, error and delufion. Therefore, a time of eminent holinefs, muft be a time of proportionably great light and knowledge. This is the reprefentation which the fcripture gives of that time. The end of binding fatan, and cafting him into the bottomlefs pit, is faid to be, " That he fhould deceive the nations no more, till the thoufand years fhould be fulfilled." This will put an end to the darknefs, and multiplicity of ftrong delufions, which do prevail, and will prevail, till that time, by which fatan fupports and promotes his intereft and kingdom among men.— Then " The face of the covering caft over all people, and the vail fpread over all nations, fhall be taken away and deftroyed :"§

H　　　　　　　　" And

---

* Ezek. xxxix. 29.　　† Joel ii. 28, 29.
‡ Acts ii. 16, &c.　　§ Ifai. xxv. 7.

" And the eyes of them that see, shall not be dim ; and the ears
of them that hear, shall hearken.    The heart also of the rash,
shall understand knowledge, and the tongue of the stammerers
shall be ready to speak plainly."*    The superior light and knowledge of that day, is metaphorically represented in the following
words :    " Moreover, the light of the  moon shall be as the light
of the sun, and the light of the sun shall be seven fold, as the light
of seven days, in the day that the Lord bindeth up the breach of
his people, and healeth the stroke of their wound."†    In that day,
" The earth shall be full of the knowledge of the Lord, as the
waters cover the sea."‡

The holy scriptures will then be attended to by all, and studied
with care, meeknefs, humility and uprightnefs of heart, earneftly
defiring to underftand them, and know the truth ; and the truths
they contain will be received with a high relifh and delight : And
the Bible will be much better underftood, than ever before.    Many
things expreffed or implied in the fcripture, which are now overlooked and difregarded, will then be difcovered, and appear important and excellent ; and thofe things which now appear intri-
cate and unintelligible, will then appear plain and eafy.    Then
public teachers will be eminently burning and fhining lights ; apt
to teach ; fcribes well inftructed into the things of the kingdom
of heaven, who will bring out of their treafures, things new and
old : And the hearers will be all attention, and receive the truth
in the love of it, into honeft and good hearts ; and light and
knowledge will conftantly increafe.    The converfation of friends
and neighbours, when they meet, will be full of inftruction, and
they will affift each other in their inquiries after the truth, and in
purfuit of knowledge.    Parents will be able and difpofed to inftruct
their children, as foon as they are capable of learning ; and they
will early underftand what are the great and leading truths which
are revealed in the Bible, and the duties and inftitutions there
prefcribed.    And from their childhood they will know and underftand the holy fcriptures, by which they will grow in underftanding and wifdom ; and will foon know more than the greateft and
beft divines have known in ages before.    And a happy foundation
will be laid for great advances in knowledge and ufefulnefs to the
end of life.    Agreeable to this, the fcripture, fpeaking of that day,
fays, " There fhall be no more thence (i. e. in the church) an in-

fant

* Ifai. xxxii. 3, 4.    † Ifai. xxx. 26.    ‡ Ifai. xi. 9.

fant of days, nor an old man that hath not filled his days.; for the child shall die an hundred years old."*    " An infant of days," is an *old infant.* That is, an old man who is an infant in knowledge, understanding and discretion. Many such aged infants have been, and still are to be found. In that day all shall make advances in true knowledge, discretion and wisdom, in some proportion to their years. " Nor an old man that hath not filled his days." That is, an old man who has not improved in knowledge and usefulness and every good attainment, according to his age. " For a child shall die an hundred years old." That is, children in years shall then make such early progress in knowledge, and in religion, and in all excellent and useful attainments, that they shall equal, if not surpass, the highest attainments in these things, of the oldest men who have lived in former ages.

They will then have every desirable advantage and opportunity to get knowledge. They will all be engaged in the same pursuit, and give all the aid and assistance to each other, in their power.— They will all have sufficient leisure to pursue and acquire learning of every kind, that will be beneficial to themselves and to society ; especially knowledge of divinity. And great advances will be made in all arts and sciences, and in every useful branch of knowledge, which tends to promote the spiritual and eternal good of men, or their convenience and comfort in this life.

III.  It will be a time of universal peace, love and general and cordial friendship. War and all strife and contention shall then cease, and be succeeded by mutual love, friendship and benificence. Those lusts of men, which originate in self love, or selfishness, which produce all the wars and strifes among men, shall be subdued and mortified, and yield to that disinterested benevolence, that heavenly wisdom, which is peaceable, gentle and easy to be intreated.  This will effectually put an end to war, as the scripture teaches.  " And he shall judge among the nations, and shall rebuke many people : And they shall beat their swords into plow-shares, and their spears into pruning hooks : Nation shall not lift up sword against nation, neither shall they learn war any more. And my people shall dwell in a peaceable habitation, and in sure dwellings, and in quiet resting places."†  The whole world of mankind will be united as one family, wisely seeking the good of

each

---

each other, in the exercife of the moft fweet love and friendfhip, founded upon the beft and everlafting principles. "The meek fhall inherit the earth, and fhall delight themfelves in the abundance of peace." This change, which fhall then take place, in which men, who were in ages before, like favage beafts, injurious, cruel, revengeful and deftructive to each other, fhall lay afide all this, and become harmlefs, humble and benevolent, is fet in a ftriking, beautiful light in prophecies, reprefenting it by the moft fierce and cruel beafts of prey, changing their nature, and living quietly with thofe creatures which they ufed to deftroy ; and fo tame and pliable that a little child might lead them ; and by the môft venomous creatures and infects becoming harmlefs, fo that a child might play with them without any danger of being hurt. Ifaiah, fpeaking of that day, fays, "The wolf fhall dwell with the lamb, and the leopard fhall lie down with the kid ; and the calf, and the young lion, and the fatling together, and a little child fhall lead them. And the cow and the bear fhall feed ; their young ones fhall lie down together : And the lion fhall eat ftraw, like the ox. And the fucking child fhall play on the hole of the afp, and the weaned child fhall put his hand on the cockatrice den."* Then "They fhall fit every man under his vine, and under his fig tree, and none fhall make them afraid."†

IV. In that day, men will not only be united in peace and love, as brethren ; but will agree in fentiments, refpecting the doctrines and truth contained in the Bible, and the religious inftitutions and practice, which are there prefcribed.

Profeffing chriftians have been from the beginning of chriftianity to this day, greatly divided, and have oppofed each other in their religious fentiments and practices ; and are now divided into various parties, fects and denominations, while all appeal to divine revelation, and profefs to take their fentiments and practices from that.

It has been often faid by fome profeffing chriftians, and is a fentiment which appears to be fpreading at this day, That difference in religious fentiments, and in attendance on the inftitutions of the gofpel, and modes of worfhip, is attended with no inconvenience, but is rather defirable, and advantageous ; and by this variety, chriftianity is rendered more agreeable and beautiful.

That

* Ifai. xi. 6, 7, 8.      † Mic. iv. 4.

That it is impoffible that all men, whofe capacities and genius are
fo different and various, and their minds, and way of thinking and
conception are naturally fo far from being alike, fhould ever be
brought to think alike, and embrace the fame religious fentiments.
That this difference in man's belief and fentiment cannot be
criminal ; for men are no more obliged to think alike, than they
are to look alike, and have the fame bodily features and ftature.
All the union that is required, or that can take place, is that of
kind affection, love and charity.

But fuch fentiments as thefe are not agreeable to reafon or
fcripture. Error in judgment and fentiment, efpecially in things
of a moral nature, is always wrong ; and does not confift or
originate merely in any defect of the moral faculties of the mind ;
but is of a moral nature, in which the tafte, affection, or inclination of the heart is concerned ; and therefore is always, in every
degree of it, morally wrong, and more or lefs criminal. Were
the moral faculties of the mind, were the heart, perfectly right,
man would not be capable of error, or of judging wrong, or making any miftake, efpecially in things of religion. The natural
faculties of the mind, of perception and underftanding or reafon,
confidered as feparate from the inclination or will, do not lead,
and have no tendency in themfelves, to judge wrong, or contrary
to the truth of things. To do fo, is to judge without evidence,
and contrary to it, which the mind never would or could do, were
not the inclination or heart concerned in it, fo as to have influence,
which muft be a wrong inclination, and contrary to the truth, and
to evidence ; and therefore is morally wrong, or criminal.

Therefore, all the miftakes and wrong opinions which men entertain, refpecting the doctrines, inftitutions and duties revealed in
the Bible, are criminal, and of a bad tendency. They muft be
fo, as they are contrary to man's obligation and duty to believe
all revealed truth ; and are wholly owing to a wrong bias or inclination, or the depravity and corruption of the heart. What
God has revealed in his word, he has declared to man, to be received by him, and believed to be the truth ; of which he has given
fufficient evidence. And the man who does not believe what God
has clearly revealed, and of which he has given fufficient evidence,
even all that can be reafonably defired, does abufe and pervert his
own underftanding, and fhuts his eyes againft the truth, and re-
fufes to receive the teftimony which God has given. And who
will fay there is no crime in this !                          Since

Since therefore, all mistakes and errors, contrary to the truths made known in the Bible, are criminal, and owing to the corruption of the heart of man, then perfect holiness will exclude all error, and there neither is, nor can be, any wrong judgment in heaven ; and in the Millennium, which will be a greater image of heaven than ever was before on earth, holiness, light and knowledge, will rise so high, that the former errors in principle and practice will subside, and there will be a great and general union in the belief and practice of the truth, contained in divine revelation.

As there is but " one Lord, one faith, and one baptism," so in that day men will be united in the belief and profession of this one faith, in the system of doctrines revealed in the Bible, which then will appear plain, and with the clearest evidence to all. And they will have one common Lord, will understand, and obey all the commands of Christ ; and they will know what are the institutions and ordinances which Christ has appointed, which are all implied in baptism : They will understand what is the import of this, and implied in it, and be united in sentiments and practice, so as to form a beautiful, happy union and harmony ; which will put an end to the variety and opposition of opinions, and practices, which now divide professing christians into so many sects, parties and denominations. The whole church, with all the members of it, which will fill the earth, and include all mankind then living, will in that day, come to that to which the gospel tends, and is designed to bring it : It will " Come in *the unity of the faith,* and of the knowledge of the Son of God, unto a perfect man, unto the measure of the stature of the fulness of Christ : That they shall be no more children, tossed to and fro, and carried about with every wind of doctrine, by the sleight of men, and the cunning craftiness, whereby they lie in wait to deceive : But speaking the truth in love, shall grow up into him in all things, which is the head, even Christ."[*] Then, agreeable to the wish and injunction of the Apostle Paul, christians will " all speak the same thing, and there will be no divisions among them ; but will be perfectly joined together in the same mind, and in the same judgment."[†] Then the inventions and prescriptions of men, both in doctrines and modes of worship, and in christian practice, will be abolished and cease. The Bible will be then understood, and be found a sufficient

* Eph. iv. 13, 14, 15.     † 1 Cor. i. 10.

fufficient and perfect rule of faith and practice, in which all will agree, and will join " with one mind, and one mouth, to worfhip and glorify God."\* Then the weapons of the gofpel, the truths of divine revelation, being preached, underftood and received, will caft down the imaginations of men, and every high thing, introduced by the pride of man, which now exalts itfelf againft the knowledge of God ; and will bring into captivity every thought, to the obedience of Chrift."† " And the Lord fhall be king over all the earth. In that day fhall there be one Lord, and his name one."‡ All fhall agree in their view and acknowledgment of the divine character, and confequently in all the revealed truths and dictates contained in the Bible. Chrift will then come to his temple, his church, " and he will be like a refiner's fire, and like fuller's foap. And he fhall fit as a refiner and purifier of filver ; and he fhall purify the fons of Levi, and purge them as gold and filver, that they may offer unto the Lord an offering in righteoufnefs."§ The queftion will be afked now, as it was then, " But who may abide the day of his coming ? And who fhall ftand when he appeareth ?" What fect or denomination of chriftians will abide the trial of that day, and be eftablifhed ?

Anfwer.—Nothing but the truth, or that which is conformable to it, will abide the trial of that day. " The lip of truth fhall be eftablifhed forever."‖ " The righteous nation which *keepeth the truth* fhall enter in," and be eftablifhed in that day.¶ Thofe of every denomination will doubtlefs expect, that the doctrines they hold, and their mode of worfhip and difcipline, and practice, with refpect to the inftitutions and ordinances of Chrift, will be then eftablifhed as agreeable to the truth ; and all others will be given up ; and all men will freely conform to them. But the moft, and perhaps all, will be much difappointed in this expectation ; efpecially with regard to the different modes of worfhip, and practifes relating to difcipline, and the ordinances of the gofpel. When the church comes to be built up in that day, and put on her beautiful garments, it will doubtlefs be different from any thing which now takes place ; and what church and particular denomination is now neareft the truth, and the church which will exift at that time, muft be left to be decided by the event. It is certain, that all doctrines and practices which are not agreeable to the truth, will

---

\* Rom. xv. 6.    † 2 Cor. x. 4, 5.    ‡ Zech. xiv. 9.
§ Mal. iii. 1, 2, 3.    ‖ Prov. xii. 19.    ¶ Ifai. xxvi. 2.

will at that day, as wood, hay, and ftubble, be burnt up. Therefore, it now highly concerns all, honeftly to feek and find, love and practife, truth and peace.

It is agreeable to human nature, and feems to be effential to rational creatures, to be moft pleafed with thofe who think as they do, and are of the fame fentiments with themfelves, in thofe things in which they feel themfelves chiefly interefted and concerned. And this agreement in fentiment, cements and increafes their union and friendfhip. But this is true, in a peculiar fenfe and degree, in the cafe before us. There can be no proper, cordial, religious union among profeffing chriftians, who wholly differ and oppofe each other in their opinion, refpecting the truths and doctrines of the gofpel. And agreement in fentiment, and in the knowledge and belief of the truth, is effential to the moft happy chriftian union and friendfhip. To him who loves the truth, error in others is difagreeable and hateful, and that in proportion to the degree of his love of the truth, and pleafure in it. Therefore, chriftians love one another *in the truth*, as the Apoftles and primitive chriftians did. " The Elder, unto the well beloved Gaius, whom I love in the truth."\* Where there is no agreement and union in fentiment, and belief of the truth, there is no foundation for chriftian love and friendfhip. Love, without any regard to truth, is not chriftian love. In this fenfe, the knowledge and belief of the truth, and chriftian love, cannot be feparated : And where there is no knowledge and belief of the truths of the gofpel, and agreement in fentiment, there can be no union of heart, and true chriftian love and friendfhip. †

As

---

\* 3 John, verfe 1.

† They who talk of chriftian union, love and charity, where there is no agreement in fentiment, refpecting the truths and doctrines of the gofpel, but a great difference and oppofition; and think that doctrinal fentiments are of no importance in chriftianity ; and that their having no belief of particular doctrines, and no creed; or differing in their religious fentiments ever fo much, is no impediment to the greateft union and chriftian friendfhip, feem not to know, what real chriftian union, love and friendfhip is. It is certain they do not love one another *in the truth*, and *for the truth's fake*, which dwelleth in them, as chriftians did in the Apoftles days, 2 John 1, 2. The catholicifm and love for which they plead, appears to be a *political* love and union, which may in fome meafure unite civil worldly focieties ; but has nothing of the nature of real chriftianity, and that union and love by which the followers of Chrift are ONE.

As light and knowledge will be greatly increafed in the Millennium, and the great truths and doctrines contained in divine revelation will then be more clearly difcerned, and appear in their true connection, excellence and importance, they will be underftood and cordially embraced by all; and they will be united together in the fame mind, and the fame judgment; and by this be formed to a high degree of happy chriftian union, love and friendfhip, loving one another in the truth, with a pure heart fervently. Thus were the primitive chriftians united in knowing and obeying the truth, whom the Apoftle Peter thus addreffes : "Seeing ye have purified your fouls in *obeying the truth* through the Spirit, unto unfeigned love of the brethren ; fee that ye love one another with a pure heart fervently."* In that day the promife and prophecy fpoken by Jeremiah, will be accomplifhed, to a greater extent and degree than it ever was before. "And I will give them one heart, and *one way*, that they may fear me forever, for the good of them, and of their children after them."†

V. THE Millennium will be a time of great enjoyment, happinefs and univerfal joy.

This is often mentioned in prophecy, as what will take place in that day, in a peculiar manner and high degree. "For ye fhall go out with joy, and be led forth with peace : The mountains and the hills fhall break forth before you into finging, and all the trees of the field fhall clap their hands. Be you glad, and rejoice forever in that which I create ; for I create Jerufalem a rejoicing, and her people a joy."‡ The enjoyments of that day are reprefented by a rich and plentiful feaft for all people, confifting in provifion of the moft agreeable and delicious kind. "And in this mountain fhall the Lord of hofts make unto all people a feaft of fat things, a feaft of wines on the lees, a feaft of fat things full of marrow, of wines on the lees well refined."§ The enjoyments and happinefs of the Millennium, are compared to a marriage fupper. "Let us rejoice and give honour to him : For the marriage of the Lamb is come, and his wife hath made herfelf ready. Bleffed are they who are called unto the marriage fupper of the Lamb."‖ And there will be a great increafe of happinefs and joy in heaven, at the introduction of that day, and during the continuance of it."¶

I                                                    " There

---

* 1 Pet. i. 22.    † Jer. xxxii. 39.    ‡ Ifai. lv. 12, lxv. 18.
§ Ifai. xxv. 6.    ‖ Rev. xix. 7, 9.    ¶ Rev. xviii. 20. xix. 1—7.

" There fhall be joy in heaven, and there is joy in the prefence of the angels of God, over one finner that repenteth."*

And this great increafe of happinefs and joy on earth will be the natural and even neceffary confequence, of the great degree and univerfality of knowledge and holinefs, which all will then profefs. The knowledge of God, and the Redeemer, and love to him, will be the fource of unfpeakable pleafure and joy in his charaᴄter, government and kingdom. And the more the great truths of divine revelation are opened and come into view, and the wifdom and grace of God in the work of redemption, are feen ; the more they are contemplated and relifhed, the greater will be their enjoyment and happinefs ; and great will be their evidence and affurance of the love and favour of God, and that they fhall enjoy him, and all the bleffings and glory of his kingdom forever.— Then, as it is prediᴄted of that time, " The work of righteoufnefs fhall be peace, and the effeᴄt of righteoufnefs, quietnefs and affurance forever."† Then the eminent degree of righteoufnefs or holinefs, to which all fhall arrive, will be attended with great enjoyment and happinefs, which is often meant by *peace* in fcripture. And the effeᴄt and confequence of this high degree of holinefs, and happinefs, in feeing and loving God and divine truth, fhall be, that they fhall have a fteady, quiet affurance of the love of God, and of his favour forever, which will greatly add to their happinefs.‡

They will have unfpeakable fatisfaᴄtion and delight in worfhipping God in fecret, and in focial worfhip, whether more private or public. And their meditations and ftudy on divine things will be fweet. The word of God will be to them fweeter than honey or the honey comb ; and they will rejoice in the truths there revealed,

---

* Luke xv. 7, 10,　　　† Ifai. xxxii. 17.

‡ Note. Affurance of the love of God, and of enjoying his favour forever, is here faid to be the *effeᴄt* of the exercife of holinefs, and that peace of foul and enjoyment which attends it : So that perfons muft *firft* be holy, and love God, *before* they can have any affurance or evidence that God loves them, and that they fhall be faved ; the latter being the effeᴄt, and not the caufe of the former. They therefore turn things upfide down, and contradiᴄt this paffage, and the whole of divine revelation, and even all reafon and common fenfe, who hold that perfons muft *firft* have affurance, or at leaft believe, that God loves them, with an everlafting love, *before* they can love God, or exercife any degree of true holinefs : And that the latter is the effeᴄt of the former !

revealed, more than the men of the world ever did, or can do in all riches. In public affemblies, while the heart and lips of the preacher will glow with heavenly truth, and he pours light and inftruction on a numerous congregation, they will all hang upon his lips, and drink in the divine fentiments which are communicated, with a high relifh and delight. And in fuch entertainments there will be enjoyed unfpeakably more real pleafure and happinefs, than all the men of the world ever found in the moft gay, brilliant company, with the moft agreeable feftivity and mirth, mufic and dancing, that is poffible. The latter is not worthy to be compared with the former.

Then religious enjoyment, whether in company or alone, will appear to be a reality, and of the higheft and moft noble kind ; and every one will be a witnefs and inftance of it. There will then be no briar and thorns to moleft enjoyment, or render company difagreeable ; but all will be amiable, happy and full of love, and render themfelves agreeable to every one. Every one will behave with decency and propriety towards all, agreeable to his ftation and connections. The law of kindnefs will be on the tongues of all ; and true friendfhip, of which there is fo little among men now, will then be common and univerfal, even chriftian love and friendfhip, which is the moft excellent kind of friendfhip, and is indeed the only real, happy, lafting friendfhip. And this will lay a foundation for a peculiar, happy intimacy and friendfhip, in the neareft relations and connections : By which conjugal and domeftic duties will be faithfully performed ; and the happinefs of thofe relations will be very great ; and the end of the inftitutions of marriage, and families, be anfwered in a much greater degree, than ever before, and they will have their proper effect, in promoting the enjoyment of individuals, and the good of fociety.

Then the happinefs and joy each one will have in the welfare of others, and the bleffings beftowed on them, will be very great. Now the few chriftians who exercife difinterefted benevolence, have, as the Apoftle Paul had, great heavinefs, and continual forrow in their hearts, while they behold fo many miferable objects : And are furrounded with thofe who are unhappy in this world, and appear to be going to everlafting deftruction, by their folly and obftinacy in fin. They have great comfort and joy, indeed, in the few who appear to be chriftians, and heirs of eternal life.— When they fee perfons who appear to underftand and love the

doctrines

doctrines of the gospel, and to have imbibed the amiable, excellent spirit of christianity, and to be the blessed favourites of heaven, they greatly rejoice with them in their happiness, and can say, as Paul did, " What thanks can we render to God for you, for all the joy wherewith we rejoice _for your fakes_ before our God !"* But in the Millennium, the happiness and joy of each one, will be unspeakably greater, in the character and happiness of all. The benevolence of every one will be gratified and pleased to a very high degree, by all whom he beholds, all with whom he converses, and of whom he thinks ; and in their amiable character, and great happiness, he will have pleasure and joy, in proportion to the degree of his benevolence, which will vastly surpass that degree of it, which the best christians now exercise. There will then be no such infinitely miserable objects, which are now every where to be seen, to excite painful grief and sorrow ; and the character of christians will then be much more beautiful and excellent, than that of real christians is now, as they will abound so much more in all holy exercise and practice ; and their present enjoyment, and future happiness in heaven, will be more evident and realized by each one, which will give pleasure and joy to every one, in the amiable character and happiness of others, even beyond all our present conceptions. " There shall be no more a pricking briar unto the church, or particular christians, nor any grieving thorn, of all that are round about them."† But all will live in pleasing harmony and friendship ; and every one will consider himself as surrounded with amiable friends, though he may have no particular connection or acquaintance with them, and all he will see or meet as he passes in the public streets, or elsewhere, will give him a peculiar pleasure, as he will have good reason to consider them to be friends to Christ, and to him, and as professing the peculiarly amiable character of christians : And this pleasure will be mutual between those who have no particular knowledge of each other. But this enjoyment and pleasure will rise much higher between those who are particularly acquainted with each others character, exercises and circumstances ; and especially those who are in a more near connection with each other, and whose circumstances and opportunities, lead them to form and cultivate a peculiar intimacy and friendship.

But it is not to be supposed that we are now able to give a proper and full description, or to form an adequate idea of the happiness, pinefs, joy and glory of that day ; but all that is attempted, and our moft enlarged and pleafing conceptions, fail much fhort of the truth, which cannot be fully known, till that happy time fhall come. They who now have the beft and higheft tafte for divine truth, and the greateft religious enjoyment, who abound moft in chriftian love, and have the moft experience of the happinefs of chriftian friendfhip, and attend moft to the Bible, and ftudy the predictions of that day, will doubtlefs have the cleareft view of it, and moft agreeable to the truth, and the higheft fatisfaction and pleafure, in the profpect of it.

There are many other things and circumftances which will take place in that day, which are implied in what has now been obferved, or may be inferred from it, and from the fcripture, by which the advantages, happinefs and glory of the Millennium will be promoted ; fome of which will be mentioned in the following particulars :

1. All outward worldly circumftances will then be agreeable and profperous, and there will be for all, a fufficiency and fulnefs of every thing needed for the body, and for the comfort and convenience of every one.

This may be inferred from many paffages of fcripture, which refer to that day ; among which are the following : " Then fhall the earth yield her increafe ; and God, even our own God, fhall blefs us."* " Then fhall he give the rain of thy feed ; that thou fhalt fow the ground withal, and bread of the increafe of the earth, and it fhall be fat and plenteous : In that day fhall thy cattle feed in large paftures. The oxen likewife, and the young affes that ear the ground, fhall eat clear provender, which hath been winnowed with the fhovel and with the fan. And the inhabitant fhall not fay, I am fick. And they fhall build houfes, and inhabit them ; and they fhall plant vineyards, and eat the fruit of them. They fhall not build, and another inhabit ; they fhall not plant, and another eat : For as the days of a tree, are the days of my people, and mine elect fhall long enjoy the work of their hands. They fhall not labour in vain, nor bring forth for trouble : For they are the feed of the bleffed of the Lord, and their offfpring with them."† " They fhall fit every man under his vine, and

* Pfalms lxvii. 6.

† Ifai. xxx. 23, 24. xxxiii. 24. lxv. 21, 22, 23. Ezek. xxxiv. 23—27.

and under his fig tree, and none fhall make him afraid."\* " The feed fhall be profperous, the vine fhall give her fruit, and the ground fhall give her increafe, and the heavens fhall give their dew ; and I will caufe the remnant of this people to poffefs all thefe things."†

This plenty, and fulnefs of the things of this life, and worldly profperity, by which all will be in eafy, comfortable circum- ftances, as to outward conveniences, and temporal enjoyment, will be owing to the following things :

1. To the kindnefs and peculiar bleffing of God in his provi- dence. When all the inhabitants of the world fhall become emi- nently pious, and devote all they have or can enjoy in this world, to God, to the reigning Saviour, he will fmile upon men in his providence, and blefs them in the city, and in the field, in the fruit of the ground, in the increafe of their herds, and of their flocks, in their bafket and in their ftore, as he promifed he would blefs the children of Ifrael, if they would be obedient to him.‡ There will be no more unfuitable feafons or calamitous events, to pre- vent or deftroy the fruits of the earth ; but every circumftance with regard to rains and the fhining of the fun, heat and cold, will be fo ordered, as to render the earth fertile, and fucceed the labour of man in cultivating it : And there will be nothing to devour and deftroy the fruit of the field.

2. To the great degree of benevolence, virtue and wifdom, which all will then have and exercife, with refpect to the affairs of this world. There will then be no war to impoverifh, lay wafte and deftroy. This has been a vaft expenfe and fcourge to man- kind in all ages, by which poverty and diftrefs have been fpread among all nations ; and the fruits of the earth, produced and ftored by the hard labour of man, have been devoured, and worfe than loft. Then there will be no unrighteous perfons, who fhall be difpofed to invade the rights and property of others, or deprive them of what juftly belongs to them ; but every one fhall fecurely fit under his own vine, and fig tree ; and there fhall be none to make him afraid. Then there will be no law fuits, which now, in civilized nations, are fo vexatious and very expenfive of time and money. Then, by the temperance in all things, which will be practifed, and the prudent and wife care of the body, and by the fmiles of heaven, there will be no expenfive, diftreffing, de-
folating

---

\* Mich. iv. 4.   † Zech. viii. 12.   ‡ Deut. xxviii. 1—8.

folating peftilence and ficknefs; but general health will be enjoyed; by which much expenfe of time and money will be prevented.

The intemperance, excefs, extravagance and wafte, in food and raiment, and the ufe of the things of life, which were before practifed, will be difcarded and ceafe, in that day. By thefe, a great part of the productions of the earth, which are for the comfort and convenience of man, are now wafted and worfe than loft, as they are, in innumerable inftances, the caufe of debility of body, ficknefs and death. But every thing of this kind will be ufed with great prudence and economy; and in that way, meafure and degree, which will beft anfwer the ends of food, drink and clothing, and all other furniture, fo as to be moft comfortable, decent and convenient, and in the beft manner furnifh perfons for their proper bufinefs and duty. Nothing will be fought or ufed to gratify pride inordinate, fenfual appetite or luft : So that there will be no wafte of the things of life : Nothing will be loft.

And at that time, the art of hufbandry will be greatly advanced, and men will have fkill to cultivate and manure the earth, in a much better and more eafy way, than ever before; fo that the fame land will then produce much more than it does now, twenty, thirty, fixty, and perhaps an hundred fold more. And that which is now efteemed barren, and not capable of producing any thing, by cultivation, will then yield much more, for the fuftenance of man and beaft, than that which is moft productive now : So that a very little fpot will then produce more of the neceflaries and comforts of life, than large tracts of land do now. And in this way, the curfe which has hitherto been upon the ground, for the rebellion of man, will be in a great meafure removed.

There will alfo doubtlefs, be great improvement and advances made in all thofe mechanic arts, by which the earth will be fubdued and cultivated, and all the neceffary and convenient articles of life, fuch as all utenfils, clothing, buildings, &c. will be formed and made, in a better manner, and with much lefs labour, than they now are. There may be inventions and arts of this kind, which are beyond our prefent conception. And if they could be now known by any one, and he could tell what they will be, they would be thought by moft, to be utterly incredible and impoffible ; as thofe inventions and arts, which are now known and familiar to us, would have appeared to thofe who lived before they were found out and took place. It

It is not impoffible, but very probable, that ways will yet be found out by men, to cut rocks and ftones into any fhape they pleafe ; and to remove them from place to place, with as little labour, as that with which they now cut and remove the fofteft and lighteft wood, in order to build houfes, fences, bridges, paving roads, &c. And thofe huge rocks and ftones, which now appear to be ufelefs, and even a nuifance, may then be found to be made, and referved by him who is infinitely wife and good, for great ufefulnefs, and important purpofes. Perhaps there is good reafon not to doubt of this. And can he doubt of it, who confiders what inventions and arts have taken place in latter ages, which are as much an advance beyond what was known or thought of in ages before, as fuch an art would be, beyond what is now known and practifed ? The art by which they removed great ftones, and raifed them to a vaft height, by which they built the pyramids in Egypt ; and that by which huge ftones were cut and put into the temple of Jerufalem, is now loft, and it cannot be conceived how this was done. This art may be revived in the Millennium ; and there may be other inventions and arts, to us, inconceivably greater and more ufeful than that. Then, in a literal fenfe, The vallies fhall be filled, and the mountains and hills fhall be made low, and the crooked fhall be made ftraight, and the rough ways fhall be made fmooth, to render travelling more convenient and eafy, and the earth more productive and fertile.

When all thefe things are confidered, which have now been fuggefted, and others which will naturally occur to them who attend to this fubject, it will appear evident, that in the days of the Millennium, there will be a fulnefs and plenty of all the neceffaries and conveniences of life, to render all much more eafy and comfortable, in their worldly circumftances and enjoyments, than ever before, and with much lefs labour and toil : And that it will not be then neceffary for any men or women to fpend all, or the greateft part of their time in labour, in order to procure a living, and enjoy all the comforts and defirable conveniencies of life. It will not be neceffary for each one, to labour more than two or three hours in a day, and not more than will conduce to the health and vigour of the body. And the reft of their time they will be difpofed to fpend in reading and converfation, and in all thofe exercifes which are neceffary and proper, in order to improve their minds, and make progrefs in knowledge ; efpecially in the knowledg

ledge of divinity : And in ftudying the fcriptures, and in private and
focial and public worfhip, and attending on public inftruction, &c.
When the earth fhall be all fubdued, and prepared in the beft manner for cultivation, and houfes and inclofures, and other neceffary
and convenient buildings fhall be erected, and completely finifhed,
confifting of the moft durable materials, the labour will not be
hard, and will require but a fmall portion of their time, in order to
fupply every one with all the neceffaries and conveniences of live :
And the reft of their time will not be fpent in diffipation or idlenefs,
but in bufinefs, more entertaining and important, which has been
now mentioned.

And there will be then fuch benevolence and fervent charity in
every heart, that if any one fhall be reduced to a ftate of want by
fome cafuality, or by inability to provide for himfelf, he will have
all the relief and affiftance that he could defire ; and there will
be fuch a mutual care and affiftance of each other, that all worldly
things will be in a great degree, and in the beft manner common ;
fo as not to be withheld from any who may want them ; and
they will take great delight in miniftering to others and ferving
them, whenever, and in whatever ways, there fhall be opportunity
to do it.

2. In that day, mankind will greatly multiply and and increafe
in number, till the earth fhall be filled with them.

When God firft made mankind, he faid to them, " Be fruitful,
and multiply, and replenifh, (or fill) the earth, and fubdue it."*
And he renewed this command to Noah and his fons, after the
flood, and in them to mankind in general. " And God bleffed
Noah and his fons, and faid unto them, Be fruitful, and multiply,
and replenifh the earth."† This command has never yet been
obeyed by mankind ; they have yet done but little, compared
with what they ought to have done, in fubduing and filling the
earth. Inftead of this, they have fpent great part of their time
and ftrength in fubduing and deftroying each other ; and in that
impiety, intemperance, folly and wickednefs, which have brought
the divine judgments upon them ; and they have been reduced and
deftroyed in all ages by famine, peftilence and poverty, and innumerable calamities and evil occurrents ; fo that by far the greateft
part of the earth remains yet unfubdued, and lies wafte without
inhabitants. And where it has been moft fubdued and cultivated

K                                                      and

* Gen. i. 28.          † Gen. ix. i.

and populous, it has been, and ftill is, far from being filled with
inhabitants, fo that it could fupport no more, except in a very few
inftances, if in any.   An exact calculation cannot be made ; but
it is prefumed that every man, who confiders the things which
have been mentioned above, will be fenfible that this earth may
be made capable of fuftaining thoufands to one of mankind who
now inhabit it ; fo that if each one were multiplied to many thoufands, the earth would not be more than filled, and all might have
ample provifion for their fuftenance, convenience and comfort.—
This will not take place, fo long as the world of mankind continue to exercife fo much felfifhnefs, unrighteoufnefs and impiety
as they do now, and always have done :  But there is reafon to
think they will be greatly diminifhed, by their deftroying themfelves, and one another, and by remarkable divine judgments,
which will be particularly confidered in a following fection.

But when the Millennium fhall begin, the inhabitants which
fhall then be on the earth, will be difpofed to obey the divine command, to fubdue the earth, and multiply, until they have filled it ;
and they will have fkill, and be under all defirable advantages to do
it ; and the earth will be foon replenifhed with inhabitants, and be
brought to a ftate of high cultivation and improvement, in every
part of it, and will bring forth abundantly for the full fupply of
all ; and there will be many thoufand times more people than ever
exifted before at once in the world.   Then the following prophecy, which relates to that day, fhall be fulfilled : " A little one fhall
become a thoufand, and a fmall one a ftrong nation.   I the Lord
will haften it in his time."*   And there is reafon to think the
earth will be then, in fome degree, enlarged in more ways than
can now be mentioned, or thought of.   In many thoufands,
hundred of thoufands, yea, millions of inftances, large tracts now
covered with water, coves and arms of the fea, may be drained,
or the water fhut out by banks and walls ; fo that hundreds of
millions of perfons may live on thofe places, and be fuftained by
the produce of them, which are now overflowed with water.—
Who can doubt of this, who recollects how many millions of
people now inhabit Holland and the Low Countries, the greateft
part of which was once covered with the fea, or thought not to be
capable of improvement ?  Other inftances might be mentioned.

Though there will be fo many millions of millions of people
on the earth at the fame time, this will not be the leaft inconveni-

ence

ence to any ; but the contrary ; for each one will be fully ſupplied with all he wants, and they will all be united in love, as brethren of one family, and will be mutual helps and bleſſings to each other. They will die, or rather fall aſleep, and paſs into the inviſible world ; and others will come on the ſtage in their room. But death then will not be attended with the ſame calamitous and terrible circumſtances as it has been, and is now ; and will not be conſidered as an evil. It will not be brought on with long and painful ſickneſs, or be accompanied with any great diſtreſs of body or mind. They will be in all reſpects ready for it, and welcome it with the greateſt comfort and joy. Every one will die at the time, and in the manner which will be beſt for him, and all with whom he is connected : And death will not bring diſtreſs on ſurviving relatives and friends ; and they will rather rejoice than mourn, while they have a lively ſenſe of the wiſdom and goodneſs of the will of God, and of the greater happineſs of the inviſible world, to which their beloved friends are gone ; and where they expect ſoon to arrive. So that in that day, death will in a great meaſure looſe his ſting, and have the appearance of a friend, and be welcomed by all as ſuch.

3. In the Millennium, all will probably ſpeak *one language* : So that one language ſhall he known and underſtood all over the world, when it ſhall be filled with inhabitants innumerable.

The whole earth was once, and originally of one language, and. of one ſpeech.* And the folly and rebellion of men was the occaſion of their being confounded in ſpeaking and underſtanding this one language, and the introduction of a variety of languages. This was conſidered as in itſelf a great calamity, and was ordered as ſuch : And it can be conſidered in no other light. Had men been diſpoſed to improve the advantages of all ſpeaking and underſtanding one language, to wiſe and good purpoſes, this diverſity never would have taken place. And when men ſhall become univerſally pious, virtuous and benevolent, and be diſpoſed to uſe ſuch an advantage and bleſſing as having one ſpeech and language will be, for the glory of God and the general good, it will doubtleſs be reſtored to them again. This may eaſily and ſoon be done, without a miracle, when mankind and the ſtate of the world ſhall be ripe for it. When they ſhall all become as one family in affection, and diſcerning and wiſdom ſhall preſide and govern in all

K 2                                                          their

* Gen. xi. 1, 6.

their affairs, they will foon be fenfible of the great difadvantage of being divided into fo many different tongues, which will greatly impede that univerfal free intercourfe which will be very defirable ; and of the advantage of all fpeaking and ufing one language. And God may fo order things in his providence that it will then be eafy for the moft learned and wife to determine which is the beft language to be adopted, to be univerfally taught and fpoken.— And when this fhall be once determined, and publifhed through the world, by thofe who are acknowledged to be the wifeft men, and beft able to fix upon a language that fhall be univerfal, and have a right to do it, all will freely confent to the propofal. And that language will be taught in all fchools, and ufed in public writings, and books that fhall be printed ; and in a few years will become the common language, underftood and fpoken by all ; and all or moft of the different languages now in the world will be forgotten and loft. All the learning and knowledge of former ages, contained in books, in different languages, worth preferving, will be introduced and publifhed in the univerfal language, and communicated to all. This will in a great meafure, fuperfede and render ufelefs the great expenfe of time, toil and money, which is now beftowed on teaching and ftudying what are called the *learned languages.* Many thoufands if not millions of youths are now confuming years in learning thefe languages, at great expenfe of money : And thoufands of teachers are fpending their lives in attending to them. It is thought by many now, that this is a ufelefs and imprudent wafte of time and money, in moft inftances, at leaft : It will appear to be much more fo, when there fhall be one univerfal language, which fhall be underftood and fpoken by all ; and when the books written in that language fhall contain all the ufeful learning and knowledge in the world ; and all farther improvements will be communicated to the world in that language.

And when this language fhall be eftablifhed, and become univerfal, all the learning and wifdom in the world, will tend and ferve to improve it, and render it more and more perfect. And there can be no doubt that fuch improvements will be made that perfons will be able to communicate their ideas with more eafe and precifion, and with lefs ambiguity and danger of being mifunderftood, than could be done before.

And

And ways will be invented to learn children to read this language with propriety, and to fpell and write it with correctnefs,
with more eafe, and in much lefs time, than it is now done, and
with little labour and coft.  And ways may be invented, perhaps
fomething like the fhort hands, which are now ufed by many, by
which they will be able to communicate their ideas, and hold intercourfe and correfpondence with each other, who live in different parts of the world, with much lefs expenfe of time and labour,
perhaps an hundred times lefs, than that with which men now
correfpond.

This will alfo greatly facilitate the fpreading ufeful knowledge,
and all kinds of intelligence, which may be a benefit to mankind,
to all parts of the world ; and render books very cheap, and eafy
to be obtained by all.  There will then be no need of tranflations
into other languages, and numerous new impreffions, in order to
have the moft ufeful books read by all.  Many hundreds of thoufands of copies may be caft off by one impreffion, and fpread over
all the earth.  And the Bible, one of which, at leaft, every perfon
will have,  by printing fuch a vaft number of them at one impreffion, may be afforded much cheaper than it can be now ; even
though it fhould be fuppofed that no improvement will be made
in the art of printing, and making paper, which cannot be reafonably fuppofed ; but the contrary is much more probable, viz. that
both thefe will then be performed, in a better manner, and with
much lefs labour and expenfe, than they are now executed.  None
can doubt of this, who confider what improvements have been
made in thefe arts, fince they were firft invented.

This univerfality of language will tend to cement the world of
mankind fo as to make them *one*, in a higher degree, and to greater advantage, than otherwife could be.  This will abforb the dif-
tinctions that are now kept up between nations fpeaking different
languages, and promote a general, free communication.  It is obferved, when there was but one language in the world, that the
people were *one*.*  And this will greatly facilitate their united exertions, to effect whatever may be for the public good.

Therefore, fince there will be fo many and great advantages, in
having one univerfal language, underftood and ufed by all mankind, and it will anfwer fo many good purpofes, when men fhall
be difpofed to make a right improvement of it ; and fince it may
be fo eafily effected, when men fhall be united in piety and benevolence,

* Gen. xi. 6.

olence, and wifdom fhall reign among them ; there is reafon to
think that God will fo order things in his providence, and fo influence and turn the hearts of mankind, as in the moft agreeable
manner to introduce the beft language, to be adopted and ufed by
all, in that day, in which great and peculiar favour and bleffings
will be granted to the world, far beyond thofe which had been
given in preceding ages.   And this is agreeable to the fcripture,
which fpeaks of that day, as diftinguifhed and remarkable for the
union and happinefs of mankind, when they fhall have *one heart,
and one way*.   And this feems to be exprefsly predicted :  When
fpeaking of that time it is faid,  " Then will I turn to the people a
pure language, that they may all call upon the name of the Lord,
to ferve him with one confent."*   Thefe words have been underftood in another fenfe ; but the moft natural and confiftent
meaning feems to be, That the people fhall not then have a mixed
language, fpeaking with different tongues, which would naturally
feparate them into different parties, and render them barbarians to
each other in their worfhip :  But God will fo order things at that
time, that one language fhall be introduced and fpoken by all ;
and which fhall be more perfect, elegant and pure, free from thofe
defects, inconfiftencies, and that jargon, which before attended all,
or moft languages ; that they may all, even all mankind, call upon the name of the Lord, with one voice, and in one language, to
ferve him with one confent ; by which they fhall be united in
worfhip, and divine fervice, not only in heart, but in lip, as mankind never were before.

4. The church of Chrift will then be formed and regulated, according to his laws and inftitutions, in the moft beautiful and
pleafing order.

This is implied in what has been faid ; but is worthy of a more
particular attention.   There will then be but one univerfal, catholic church, comprehending all the inhabitants of the world,
formed into numerous particular focieties and congregations, as
fhall be moft convenient, to attend on public worfhip, and the inftitutions of Chrift.   There will be no fchifms in the church
then :  Chriftians will not be divided into various fects and denominations ; but there will be a beautiful and happy union in
fentiment, refpecting the doctrines, worfhip and inftitutions of
Chrift ; and all will be of one heart, and one way, and ferve
Chrift with one confent.   The ordinances of baptifm and the
                                                          Lord's

* Zeph. iii. 9.

Lord's fupper, and all the inftitutions of Chrift, will be attended in due order, with folemnity and decency ; and being accompanied with divine efficacy, will have their proper and faving effect. All the children will be members of the church, having the initiating feal applied to them, and being folemnly devoted to Chrift in baptifm ; and they will be faithfully brought up for him, and early difcover their love to Chrift, not only in words, but by obeying him, and attending upon all his inftitutions. The difcipline which Chrift has inftituted, will be faithfully practifed, fo far as there fhall be any occafion ; and chriftians, by watching over each other in love, and exhorting and admonifhing one another, will prevent, or immediately heal all offences. In thofe refpects, and in others not here mentioned, and perhaps not thought of, the church of Chrift will then be the beft regulated, moft beautiful and happy fociety that ever exifted, or can be formed on earth. " When the Lord fhall build up Zion, the church, he fhall appear in his glory." Then, what is predicted in the fixtieth chapter of Ifaiah, and many other prophecies of the fame event, fhall be fufilled. God fays to his church, " Arife, fhine, for thy light is come, and the glory of the Lord is rifen upon thee : Whereas thou haft been forfaken and hated, fo that no man went through thee, I will make thee an eternal excellency, the joy of many generations. I will make the place of my feet glorious. Thou fhalt alfo be a crown of glory in the hand of the Lord, and a royal diadem in the hand of thy God. Glorious things are fpoken of thee, O city of God."*

5. Then

* It has been a queftion, Whether in the Millennium, when the church fhall be thus univerfal, and be brought to fuch a well regulated, holy and happy ftate, there will be any need of civil rulers, to prefide and govern in temporal matters? It is faid, that every thing which will be neceffary of this kind, will be regulated and ordered by particular churches, and civil officers will not be needed, and will have nothing to do.

But when it is confidered, that the church of Chrift is not a worldly fociety, and has no concern with temporal matters, and the concerns of the world, confidered merely as fuch, or any farther than they are included in obedience to the laws of Chrift : And that there will be need of regulations and laws or orders, with refpect to the temporal concerns, of mankind ; it will appear proper and convenient, if not neceffary, that there fhould be wife men chofen and appointed to fuperintend, and direct in worldly affairs, whofe bufinefs it fhall be to confult the temporal intereft of men, and dictate thofe regulations from time to time, which fhall promote the public good, and the temporal intereft of individuals.

5. Then chriftianity will appear in its true beauty and excellence, and the nature and genuine effects of it will be more manifeft than ever before, and the truth and amiablenefs of it be exhibited in a clear and ftriking light.

Chriftianity has hitherto been generally abufed and perverted
by thofe who have enjoyed the gofpel ; and but little of the genuine fpirit and power of it has appeared among thofe who have
been called chriftians. They have, the moft of them, difobeyed
the laws of Chrift, and mifreprefented and perverted the doctrines
and inftitutions of the gofpel, to accommodate it to the gratification of their felfifhnefs, pride and worldly fpirit ; and have hated
and perfecuted one another unto death. They have divided into
innumerable fects and parties, and have not been agreed in the
doctrines and inftitutions of the gofpel ; but have embraced various and contrary opinions concerning them ; and contended a-
bout them with wrath and bitternefs. And the greateft part
of the chriftian world have been as openly vicious, as the heathen nations, if not more fo. And as the name of God was
blafphemed among the Gentiles by the wicked lives of the Jews,[*]
fo the name of Chrift has been blafphemed by infidels and others,
through the various kinds of wickednefs of thofe who have been
called chriftians. By reafon of whom, the way of truth has been
evil fpoken of."[†] But few in the chriftian world, in comparifon
with the reft, have honoured Chrift, by entering into the true
meaning and fpirit of the gofpel, loving it, and living agreeable to
it : And thofe few have been generally hidden and overlooked by
the multitude of merely nominal chriftians. And genuine chriftianity is not to be found in the faith and lives of thofe in general
who affume the name of chriftians ; but in the Bible only, fince
the moft who profefs to know Chrift, by their doctrines and
works do deny him.

But in the Millennium the fcene will be changed, and chriftianity will be underftood and acted out, in the true fpirit and
power of it, and have its genuine effect, in the lives and conduct
of all. And when it comes to be thus reduced to practice by all,
it will appear from fact and experience, to have a divine ftamp ;
and that the gofpel is indeed the wifdom of God, and the power
of God, forming all who cordially embrace it to a truly amiable
and excellent character, and is fuited to make men happy in this
world,

* Rom. ii. 24.    † 2 Pet. ii. 2.

world, and that which is to come. Then all the difgrace and
reproach, which has come upon Chrift, his true followers, and
upon chriftianity, by the wickednefs and enmity of men, and the
abufe of the gofpel, fhall be wiped off. This is foretold in the
following words : " Behold, at that time I will undo all that afflict
thee, and I will fave her that halteth, and gather her that was
driven out, and I will get them praife and fame in every land,
where they have been put to fhame. ⁂ I will make you a name
and a praife among all people of the earth."* After the various
fchemes of falfe religion and infidelity have been tried by men, and
the evil nature and bad effects of them difcovered, real chriftianity,
as it is ftated in divine revelation, when it fhall be underftood by
all, and appear in univerfal practice, will fhine with peculiar luftre
and glory ; and the beauty and excellence of it, and the happinefs
it produces, will be more apparent and affecting, and be more ad-
mired, by the contraft, than if no fuch delufion and falfe religion
had taken place. This is reprefented in the laft words of David
the Prophet. " And he fhall be as the light of the morning, when
the fun rifeth, even a morning without clouds ; as the tender
grafs fpringing out of the earth by clear fhining after rain."†—
When the fun rifes in a clear morning, after a dark, ftormy night,
and the tender grafs fprings up frefh and lively, it is much more
pleafant and refrefhing, than if it had not been preceded by fuch
a night.

6. The time of the Millennium will be in a peculiar and eminent fenfe and degree, *The day of falvation*, in which the Bible, and
all the doctrines, commands and inftitutions contained in it, will
have their proper and defigned iffue and effect ; and that which
precedes that day is preparatory to it, and fuited in the beft manner to introduce it, and render it eminently the gofpel day.

The Spirit of God will then be poured out in his glorious fulnefs, and fill the world with holinefs, and falvation, as floods
upon the dry ground. All the preceding influences of the Holy
Spirit, in converting and faving men, are but the firft fruits, which
precede the harveft, which will take place in that latter day. This
was typified in the Mofaic inftitutions. The moft remarkable
feftivals were the Paffover, the feaft of the firft fruits, and the feaft
of Tabernacles, upon which all the males in Ifrael were commanded to attend at Jerufalem. The Paffover typified the death

L                                              of

* Zeph. xix. 20.              † 2 Sam. xxiii. 4.

of Chrift, and he was crucified at the time of that feaft. The
feaft of the firft fruits, or Pentecoft, as it is called in the New
Teftament, typified the firft fruits of the death of Chrift, in the
outpouring of the Holy Spirit, and the converfion of men, when
the gofpel was firft preached, which took place at the time of this
feaft."* The feaft of Tabernacles, which was "the feaft of *ingathering*, which was in the end of the year ;"† was a type of the
Millennium, which will be in the latter end of the world, when
the great and chief ingathering of fouls to Chrift and his church,
fhall take place. This is the time when Chrift will fee the fruit
of the travel of his foul, and fhall be fatisfied. To this day moft
of the prophecies of Chrift, and falvation, and of the good things
which were coming to the church, have their principal reference,
and they will have their chief fulfilment then. This is the day
which our Lord faid Abraham faw with gladnefs and joy. "Your
father Abraham rejoiced (or leaped forward) to fee my day : And
he faw it, and was glad."‡ He faw the day of Chrift in the
promife made to him, That in his feed all nations fhould be bleffed ; which will be accomplifhed in the Millennium, and not before. This is the day of Chrift, the day of his great fuccefs and
glory. This is the gofpel day, in comparifon with which all that
precedes it, is night and darknefs.

Then the chief end of divine revelation will be anfwered. It
has been given with a chief reference to that time, and it will then
be the mean of producing unfpeakably greater good, than in all
ages before. It will then be no longer mifunderftood, and perverted and abufed, to fupport error and wickednefs ; but be univerfally prized more than all riches, and improved to the beft purpofes, as the fountain of knowledge and wifdom. And all the
inftitutions and ordinances appointed by Chrift, will then have
their chief effect. They will then be underftood and take place
in due order, and be attended in a proper manner ; and the wifdom and goodnefs of Chrift in ordaining them, will be feen and
experienced by all. Then the gofpel will be preached, as it never
was before, fince the days of infpiration ; in which the minifters of the gofpel will be eminently burning and fhining lights,
exhibiting the important, affecting, glorious truths of the gofpel,
in a clear and ftriking light, and in a manner moft agreeable and
entertaining ; which will fall into honeft and good hearts, and
be

* Acts ii. 1.          † Exod. xxxiv. 22.          ‡ John viii. 56.

be received with the higheft relifh and pleafure, and bring forth fruit abundantly. The Sabbath will be a moft pleafant and profitable day, and improved to the beft and moft noble purpofes. And the adminiftration of baptifm and the Lord's fupper, according to divine inftitution, will greatly conduce to the edification of the church, and appear in their true importance and ufefulnefs, as they never did before ; thefe and all other inftitutions of Chrift, being appointed with fpecial reference to that day, when they will have their chief ufe, and anfwer the end of their appointment.

As the winter in the natural world is preparatory to the fpring and fummer, and the rain and fnow, the fhining of the fun, the wind and froft, iffue in the order, beauty and fruitfulnefs of the vegetable world ; and have their proper effect in thefe ; and the end of winter is anfwered chiefly in what takes place in the fpring and fummer, and the former is neceffary to introduce the latter, and in the beft manner to prepare for it : So in the moral world, or the church of Chrift, what precedes the Millennium is as the winter, while the way is preparing for the fummer, and all that takes place has reference to that happy feafon, and is fuited to introduce it in the beft manner and moft proper time, when the gofpel, fo far as it refpects the church in this world, and all the inftitutions and ordinances of it, will have their genuine and chief effect, in the order, beauty, felicity and fruitfulnefs of the church.

## S E C T I O N III.

*In which is confidered which thoufand years of the world will be the Millennium, and when it will begin.*

ALL who attend to the fubject of the Millennium, will naturally inquire, When this happy time will take place ; and how long it will be before it fhall be introduced ? And fome who have undertaken to find from fcripture, and to tell the precife time and the year when it will begin, have been evidently miftaken,

taken, becaufe the time on which they fixed for this, is paffed, and
the event has not taken place. From this, fome have concluded,
that it is uncertain whether there will ever be fuch a time ; and
others have exploded all attempts to find from fcripture when
this time will be.

Though there be good reafon to conclude that the exact time,
the particular day or year, of the beginning of the Millennium
cannot be known, and that it will be introduced gradually, by
different fucceffive great and remarkable events, the precife time
of which cannot be known before they take place ; and that the
prophecies refpecting it, are fo formed on defign, that no man
can certainly know when the event predicted fhall be accomplifhed, within a year, or a number of years, until it is manifeft by
the accomplifhment, as fuch knowledge would anfwer no good
end, but the contrary : Yet there is no reafon to fuppofe that this
is left wholly in the dark, and that it is impoffible to know, within
a thoufand, or hundreds of years, when this glorious day fhall
commence, which is fo much the fubject of prophecy, in which
the glory which is to follow the fufferings of Chrift, and the afflictions of his church, will chiefly confift, fo far as it relates to the
tranfactions of time.

Though it may be evident from fcripture, that the feventh
thoufand years of the world, will be the time of the profperity of
the church of Chrift, on earth ; yet this event may come on by
degrees, and be in a meafure introduced years before that time ;
and the church may not be brought to the moft complete and
happy ftate of that day, but ftill have farther advances to make,
after this feventh thoufand years begin, and continue fome years
after they are ended : So that the particular year of the beginning
or end of this time, cannot be known, before it actually takes
place.

It is thought that there is reafon to conclude from divine revelation, that the feventh millenary of the world, will be the time
in which the church of Chrift will enjoy a fabbath of reft, and be
brought to its higheft and chief profperity in this world, which is
fo much the fubject of fcripture prophecy ; and that the end of
the world, and the day of general judgment, will take place foon
after this Millennium is over. The following obfervations are
defigned to point out fome of the evidence of this.

It

It has been already obferved, That the creation of the natural world in fix days, and the feventh being appointed to be a day of reft, does afford an argument that the moral world, or the church and kingdom of Chrift, of which the natural world is a defigned type, in many refpects, will be fix thoufand years in forming, in order to be brought to fuch a ftate, as in the beft manner to enjoy a thoufand years of reft, peace and profperity ; a day in the natural world, in this inftance, reprefenting a thoufand years in the moral world : And that time being thus divided into *fevens*, to have a perpetual rotation to the end of it, denotes that the world is to ftand but feven thoufand years, as " One day is with the Lord as a thoufand years, and a thoufand years as one day." And that this has been handed down as the opinion of many ancients, both Jews and Chriftians.* It is acknowledged, that this argument is not fufficient to eftablifh this point, confidered by itfelf alone ; but it is thought to have fome weight, when joined with other arguments from fcripture which coincide with this, and ferve to ftrengthen it.

It is obfervable, that the number *feven* is the moft noted number mentioned in fcripture, in many refpects, and is a *facred number* above all others. And in the Mofaic ritual, which contained many typical inftitutions, the Ifraelites were commanded, not only to obferve every feventh day, as a day of reft; but every feventh year as a Sabbath, and year of reft. And the feventh month in every year, was a feftival and facred month, above all other months of the year. In this month was the feaft of Tabernacles, which was to be obferved feven days with great joy. On the firft day of this month was the feaft of trumpets, when the trumpets were to be blown through all the land, which was a type of the extraordinary preaching of the gofpel which will introduce the Millennium. And on the tenth day was their annual and moft folemn faft, on which they were to confefs their fins and afflict their fouls, and atonement was made for them. Which was a figure of the repentance and extraordinary humiliation, to which the inhabitants of the world will be brought, by the preaching of the gofpel, attended with the difpenfations of divine providence fuited to promote this, previous to their being raifed up to the profperity and joy of that day. And then the joyful feaft of ingathering, in the end of the year, came on, on the fifteenth day of the fame month.

* See Sect. I. Page 36, 37. with the note there.

month. This was a type of the happy, joyful Millennium in the seventh and last thousand years of the world, in which vast multitudes, even most of the redeemed, will be gathered into the church and kingdom of Christ; in comparison with whom, all who shall have been saved before this time, are but the first fruits of the purchase of Christ.

It is evident that this feast of Tabernacles in the seventh month, was a designed type of the Millennium, from what has been now observed, and what has been said on the three most remarkable feasts appointed in the law of Moses, in the preceding section, but this evidence is strengthened, and made certain, by what is said by the Prophet Zechariah. When he is speaking of the Millennium, and predicting that happy day, he says, " And it shall come to pass, that every one that is left of all the nations which came against Jerusalem, shall even go up from year to year to worship the King, the Lord of hosts, *and to keep the feast of Tabernacles.*"* By the feast of Tabernacles are meant the enjoyments and blessings of the Millennium, of which all nations shall then partake, and which were typified by that feast.

All these things seem to point out the seventh thousand years of the world to be the time of the Millennium. But there is yet greater evidence of this, which will serve to strengthen what has been observed, and shew that it is not mere conjecture.

The prophecies in the book of Daniel, of the rise and continuance of the little horn, and of the time in which the church shall be in a state of affliction; and those in the Revelation, of the continuance of the beast, who is the same with the horn; and of the duration of the afflicted state of the church during that time, when examined, and compared, will lead to fix on the seventh thousand years of the world to be the time of the Millennium.

In the Revelation, the time of the continuance of the beast, after his deadly wound was healed, is said to be forty and two months.† And the time in which the church should be trodden down, afflicted and oppressed, is said to be forty and two months a thousand two hundred and sixty days, and a time, and times, and half a time.‡ The same term of time is denoted by each of these expressions. A year was then reckoned to contain three hundred and sixty days; and a month consisted of thirty days. In forty and two months were a thousand two hundred and sixty days.

* Zech. xiv. 16.　　† Chap. xiii. 5.　　‡ Chap. xi. 2, 3. xii. 6, 14.

days. And a time, and times, and half a time, are three years and
a half, which contain forty and two months, and a thoufand two
hundred and fixty days.   So long the beaft, the idolatrous perfecuting power, exercifed by the Bifhop of Rome, the Pope, is to
continue; during which time, the church of Chrift is to be oppreffed, afflicted and oppofed, reprefented by the holy city being
trodden under foot by the Gentiles; the two witneffes prophecy-
ing in fackcloth ; and a woman perfecuted and flying into the
wildernefs, to hide herfelf from her enemies, where fhe is fed and
protected during the reign of the beaft, which is to continue a
thoufand two hundred and fixty years, a prophetical day being a
year.   At the end of thofe years, the Pope and the church of
Rome, of which he is the head, will be deftroyed.   And according to the reprefentation in the Revelation, the kingdom of the
devil in the world, will fall at the fame time, and the kingdom of
Chrift be fet up on the ruins of it, and the Millennium will take
place.

If it were known when the Bifhop of Rome firft became what is
defigned to be denoted by the beaft, the time of his fall, and of the
end of the church of Rome, and of fatan's kingdom in the world,
when the Millennium will commence, could not be afcertained to
a year.   But as this beaft rofe gradually from ftep to ftep, till he
became a beaft, in the higheft and moft proper fenfe, this involves
the fubject in fome degree of uncertainty, and renders it more dif-
ficult to determine, at which confiderable increafe and advance of
the Bifhop of Rome in power and influence, the thoufand two hundred and fixty years began.   He had great influence, not only in
the church, in ecclefiaftical matters, but in the temporal affairs of
the Roman empire, and of the kingdoms which were erected in it,
by the invafion of the northern nations, before he was publicly acknowledged and declared to be Univerfal Bifhop ; which was done
in the year of Chrift, 606.   This greatly increafed his influence and
power in the chriftian world; and the church was now become exceeding corrupt.   If the 1260 years be reckoned from this time,
they will end in the year 1866, feventy four years from this time,
viz. 1792.   But the Pope did not become a temporal prince, and
publicly affume civil jurifdiction, till the year 756, when Pepin,
the king of France, then the moft powerful prince in chriftendom,
made him prince over a large dominion, and he affumed civil authority, and upon this he fubdued three kings or kingdoms, and
                                                          they

they fell before him, according to the prediction of him in the prophecy of Daniel.\*    And he soon had such power over the nations, as to set up an emperor in Germany, to be his tool, by whom to raise himself to universal empire, referving to himself and claiming power over the emperor, and over all kings in the chriftian world, to fet them up and crown them, or depofe them when he pleafed.

This is the moft remarkable epoch ; when the Pope became a beaft, in the moft proper fenfe, from whence his reign is to be dated.    Twelve hundred and fixty years from this date, 756, will end near the beginning of the feventh thoufandth years of the world.    But as he rofe to this height gradually, and was a beaft in a lower fenfe long before this, it is reafonable to fuppofe that he will fall by degrees, until his ufurped power is wholly taken from him, and the falfe church of Rome, the great whore, utterly deftroyed ; and that he has been falling many years ; and that as the time of his reign draws nearer to a clofe, more remarkable events, by which he and that church will come to total ruin, will take place in a more rapid fucceffion.    But this will be more particularly confidered in the next fection.

Therefore, thefe prophecies of the rife and fall of Antichrift, or the beaft, and the time of his reign, and of the afflicted ftate of the church of Chrift, fix the end of thefe, and of the reign of fatan in the world of mankind, near the beginning of the feventh thoufand years of the world ; when the Millennium will be introduced ; though many things will take place before that time, by which the Pope and his intereft will gradually decline and fink, and in favour of the church and kingdom of Chrift, to prepare the way for the introduction of the Millennium.

In the book of Dainel, the fame idolatrous, perfecuting power, and the time of the continuance of it, and of the oppreffed ftate of the church, are predicted : And the time is fixed, and expreffed by a time, and times, and an half, or the dividing of time ; † which is the fame mentioned by St. John, in the Revelation, and is 1260 prophetic days ; that is, fo many years, as has been cbferved above.    There it is faid by him who interpreted to Daniel the vifion of the four beafts, " The fourth beaft fhall be the fourth kingdom upon earth, which fhall be divers from all kingdoms, and fhall devour the whole earth, and tread it down and break it in pieces."   This is the Roman empire.   " And the ten horns out

of

* Chap. vii. 8, 20, 24.      † Dan. vii. 25. xii. 7.

of this kingdom are ten kings that fhall arife.    And another fhall arife after them, and he fhall fubdue three kings.    And he fhall fpeak great words againft the Moft High, and fhall wear out the faints of the Moft High,  and think to change times and laws : And  they  fhall be  given into  his hand, until a time, and time, and the dividing of time.''\*    This laft horn, king or ruling power, is evidently the fame with the little  horn mentioned in the eighth chapter ;  and is the fame with the beaft when  he was  recovered to life, after he had  been  wounded unto death, which St. John faw,  that is, the Pope of Rome, in whom the power and idolatry of this  empire  is revived and continued.    The character given of each, is the fame in fubftance ;  and  the time of their continuance is the fame, which much end,  according to every probable calculation, at or about the end of the fixth thoufand years of  the world, or about two thoufand years after the incarnation of Chrift. †  And at the end  of this  time,  this power  and kingdom  is to be deftroyed, and a total end put to  the Roman empire,  reprefented by the beaft :  And the kingdom of Chrift. in its fulnefs and glory, fhall  then take place,  in the univerfal prevalence and  reign of his church and people, which is expreffed  in the following words :—  ‟ But the judgment fhall fit, and they fhall take away his dominion, to confume and deftroy it to the end.    And the kingdom and the dominion, and the greatnefs of the kingdom under the whole heaven, fhall be given to  the people of the faints of  the Moft High, whofe kingdom is an everlafting kingdom, and all dominions fhall ferve and obey him.''‡

In the eighth chapter of Daniel, we have a different reprefentation of this fame kingdom, power or empire, by a little horn which came forth out of one of the four horns, into which the Grecian empire founded by Alexander  the great, was divided,  fome time after his death.    This is  the Roman  or fourth and laft empire, upon the deftruction of which the kingdom of Chrift is to prevail, and fill the world.    Daniel defcribes this little horn, as it appeared to him in the vifion, in the following words : ‟ And  out of one of them  came  forth a little horn, which waxed exceeded great toward the fouth, and toward the eaft,  and toward the  pleafant land.    And it waxed great, even to the hoft of heaven, and it caft down fome of the hoft, and of the ftars, to the ground, and ftamped

M

upon

---

upon them. Yea, he magnified himfelf even to the prince of the
hoft, and by him the daily facrifice was taken away, and the place
of his fanctuary was caft down. And an hoft was given him
againft the daily facrifice, by reafon of tranfgreffion, and it caft
down the truth to the ground, and it practifed and profpered."*
And this vifion is explained by the angel interpreter in the following part of the chapter.† What is faid of this horn refpects the
Roman kingdom and empire, from the beginning and end of it, the
ruin of which fhall open the way for the kingdom of Chrift to flourifh in the world, and the reign of the faints on the earth. And
what is faid of this power or kingdom here, refpects the idolatry that
fhould be fupported and practifed by it, and the oppofition it
fhould make to God and his people, in which it fhould prevail,
and have power to opprefs and perfecute the faints ; and there is
fpecial reference to the Pope and thofe under his influence and
direction, when he fhould be at the head of this empire, and rule
in it, who is particularly defigned in the feventh chapter, denoted
by the little horn, " which had eyes like the eyes of man, and a
mouth fpeaking great things ; which fhould make war with the
faints, and prevail againft them ; and fpeak great words againft
the Moft High, and wear out the faints of the Moft High."‡
This power, indeed, did oppofe and deftroy the mighty and holy
people, and ftand up againft the Prince of princes, before it exifted,
and was exercifed by antichrift, in the church of Rome. Jefus
Chrift the Prince of princes, was put to death by this power.—
And this horn perfecuted the church, efpecially at times, for near
three hundred years after the death of Chrift ; all of which is
included in the defcription of the horn or kingdom, which is the
chief fubject of this chapter ; but there is particular and chief
reference to what this power would be and do, when in the hands
of antichrift, for he, above all others, has fpoken great things, and
opened his mouth to blafpheme God and the faints : He has introduced and promoted the groffeft idolatry, and ftood up againft
the Prince of princes ; has magnified himfelf in his heart even to
the Prince of the hoft, the Lord Jefus Chrift ; and has been the
moft cruel and bloody perfecutor of the faints for many ages :
He has caft down the truth to the ground, and practifed and profpered, and has deftroyed vaft numbers of the holy people, or the faints.
Gabriel, who was ordered to make Daniel underftand the vifion,
faid to him, " Behold, I will make thee know what fhall be *in the*
*laft*

---

* Verfe 9, 10, 11, 12. † Verfe 23—25. ‡ Verfe 8, 21, 25.

*laſt end of the indignation :* For at the time appointed the end ſhall be."* His interpretation had chief reſpect to the latter end of this kingdom, under the reign of antichriſt, in whoſe end the kingdom ſhould be ruined, and exiſt no more.

The queſtion is here aſked, " How long ſhall be the viſion concerning the daily ſacrifice, and the tranſgreſſion of deſolation, to give both the ſanctuary and the hoſt to be trodden under foot ?" Biſhop Newton ſays, " In the original there is no ſuch word as *concerning* ; and Mr. Lowth rightly obſerves, that the words may be rendered more agreeably to the Hebrew thus, *For how long a time ſhall the viſion laſt, the daily ſacrifice be taken away, and the tranſgreſſion of the deſolation continue,* &c. After the ſame manner the queſtion is tranſlated by the ſeventy, and in the Arabic verſion, and in the Vulgar Latin."

The anſwer is, " Unto two thouſand and three hundred days ; then ſhall the ſanctuary be cleanſed."† Theſe are no doubt prophetical days, a day being put for a year. The time therefore ſpecified is two thouſand and three hundred years. All the difficulty in fixing on the time of the end of theſe days, lies in determining at what time the reckoning begins. This is left in a degree of uncertainty, as is the beginning of the reign of antichriſt, which is to continue twelve hundred and ſixty years ; the reaſon of which doubtleſs is, that it ſhould not be preciſely known to a day or year, when this time will end, till it ſhall be actually accompliſhed, while it is made certain, the time of the end is fixed, and they who are willing to attend to the ſubject, and make uſe of all the light that is offered, may have ſufficient evidence to determine within a few years when the time will be, and not be left in a total uncertainty about it.

The little horn, which is the chief ſubject of this viſion, and was to do ſuch great things againſt the holy people, the church, came forth out of one of the four notable horns, toward the four winds of heaven, which grew out of the goat, after the one great horn was broken, which the goat had at firſt.‡ The goat is the king of Grecia, or the Grecian empire, erected by Alexander the great, who was the firſt king, or the great horn.§ After the death of Alexander, and when his ſucceſſors in his family were extinct, four kings were ſet up, and divided the great empire between them into four kingdoms, which diviſion was toward, or according

* Verſe 19.     † Verſes 13, 14.     ‡ Verſe 8.     § Verſe 21.

to the four winds, Eaſt, Weſt, North and South. Caſſander, one of the four kings, took the weſtern part of the empire, or the weſtern kingdom, containing Macedon, Greece, &c. Out of this horn came forth the little horn, which "waxed exceeding great, toward the South, and toward the Eaſt, and toward the pleaſant land."* This horn Gabriel explains to be " A king of fierce countenance, and underſtanding dark ſentences, who ſhall ſtand up."† The Romans are meant by this horn, who were weſt of Greece, and may be conſidered as included in the weſtern part of the empire, which was one of the four horns, out of which they roſe, and ſoon were conſpicuous ; and Prideaux ſays, " Their name began to grow of great note and fame among foreign nations," by their conqueſts in a few, not above five or ſix twenty years, after the above mentioned partition of the empire of the goat, into four horns or kingdoms. And they were a diſtinct people, and doubtleſs made ſome figure, when the four horns firſt exiſted. From this time, and this ſmall beginning, the Romans aroſe by their policy, power and conqueſts, until they arrived to a vaſt and univerſal empire. And as they exiſted as a people when the Grecian empire was divided into four kingdoms or horns, and they were really included in the weſtern horn, and ſoon roſe out of it, and went on and grew to univerſal empire, their beginning may properly be reckoned from the time when the weſtern horn or kingdom aroſe, in which they were included, as they ſoon after that, became a diſtinct power and kingdom, and were a little horn, and proceeded to conquer and deſtroy the horn, out of which they came, and to ſubdue all the other horns.

This partition of the Grecian empire into four kingdoms or horns, was juſt about three hundred years before the birth of Jeſus Chriſt, or the beginning of the chriſtian era. And as the incarnation of Chriſt was about the beginning of the fifth thouſand years of the world, two thouſand and three hundred years from the riſe of the four horns will end at or near the beginning of the ſeventh thouſand years of the world. Or if the beginning of the little horn ſhould not be reckoned from that time, but from the time when the Roman power or horn began to be conſpicuous and acknowledged among the nations, two thouſand three hundred years from that time, will carry them but a few years beyond the beginning of the ſeventh thouſand years of the world ,

ſo

fo that this number ferves to confirm what has been obferved from the other numbers in Daniel, and the Revelation, viz. That the reign of antichrift, who is the laft head of the Roman empire, will end about the beginning of the feventh millenary of the world, when the Millennium will begin, and the meek, the faints, fhall inherit the earth, take the kingdom and reign with Chrift.

In the laft chapter of Daniel, " One faid to the man clothed in linen, which was upon the waters of the river, How long fhall it be to the end of thefe wonders?" The anfwer is made in a very folemn manner, in the following words : " It fhall be for a time, times, and an half. And when he fhall have accomplifhed to fcatter the power of the holy people, all thefe things fhall be finifhed." He who fhall fcatter the power of the holy people or the faints, is the fame with the horn, mentioned in the feventh chapter, who fhould " Wear out the faints of the Moft High ;" which is the fame event which is here expreffed in different words. And the time of his doing this, is the fame which is mentioned here : " And they fhall be given into his hand, until a time, and times, and the dividing of time."\* That is, three prophetical years and an half, in which are 1260 prophetical days, which are put for fo many years. And this is the fame power which is called a beaft in the Revelation, who was to do the fame thing mentioned here, viz. It was given unto him to make war with the faints, and to overcome them ! And the fame time is there fixed for his doing this. " And power was given unto him to continue ( or practife and make war) forty and two months," after he was recovered to life from being wounded unto death ;† which is juft three years and an half, and twelve hundred and fixty days.

Daniel heard, but did not underftand the anfwer, and therefore put the following queftion, " Then faid I, O my Lord, what fhall be the end of thefe things?" The anfwer is, " From the time that the daily facrifice fhall be taken away, and the abomination that maketh defolate fet up, there fhall be a thoufand two hundred and ninety days. Bleffed is he that waiteth, and cometh to the thoufand three hundred and five and thirty days." Here are two different numbers or times mentioned, and neither of them agrees exactly with the foregoing anfwer. In that, the time of the continuance of the perfecuting power, which fhall fcatter and wear out the faints, is limited to 1260 years. In the anfwer to

Daniel's

---

\* Chap. vii. 25.                  † Rev. xiii. 3, 5, 7.

Daniel's queſtion, two different numbers of years are mentioned, when thofe evil things ſhall come to an end, and the prophanation of the church, and the worſhip and ordinances of Chriſt, ſhall ceafe, and the church ſhall be reſtored to due order, and be bleſſed and brought to a happy, glorious ſtate, viz. 1290, and 1335 years. The firſt is 30 years longer than the time mentioned above, and in the Revelation, and the laſt exceeds it 75 years. This feeming difference may be reconciled by obferving, that thefe anſwers do not reſpect precifely the fame event. The former expreffes the time of the continuance and reign of antichriſt, in which he ſhall opprefs the church of Chriſt : And when he ſhall have accompliſhed to fcatter the power of the holy people, he ſhall be deſtroyed. The latter looks forward to the recovery of the church of Chriſt, from her low, affliicted, broken ſtate, to a ſtate of peace and profperity, in the proper ufe and enjoyment of the worſhip, inſtitutions and ordinances of Chriſt, which had been fo greatly corrupted by the falfe church of Rome. It may take fome time to effect this, after the Pope and the church of Rome are wholly deſtroyed and extinct. As the corruption and perverſion of the church, worſhip and ordinances of Chriſt, was brought on by degrees, and conſiderable advances were made in this, after antichriſt arofe, and the Pope became a perfecuting beaſt; fo doubtlefs the church will not be wholly purified when this beaſt ſhall be deſtroyed ; but it will be fome time after this, before all corruptions and errors in doctrine and practice, will be wholly extirpated, and the church appear in her true beauty, and come to a ſtate of univerfal, eſtabliſhed peace and profperity. Within thirty years after the beaſt ſhall be ſlain, and his body deſtroyed and given to the burning flame, or at the end of 1290 years, the church may become univerfal, and all nations be members of it ; and it may arrive to a ſtate of great purity and peace, and an end be put to all her troubles, and moſt of the wicked be fwept off from the face of the earth, by fome remarkable event, and fudden ſtroke; by which the kingdom of fatan ſhall be nearly extinct ; and his influence among mankind almoſt wholly ceafe. But the church of Chriſt may not arrive to the moſt pure and happy ſtate which it ſhall enjoy, under forty or fifty years after this. For this happy period chriſtians muſt wait ; and they will be in a peculiar and high degree bleſſed, who ſhall come to this happy and glorious ſtate of the church, when the firſt refurrection ſhall be univerfal and complete, and the Millennium
ſtate

ftate eftablifhed, and brought to its full ftature, and proper height in holinefs and happinefs, which took place in a confiderable degree, and might properly be faid to have began a number of years before. But thefe events, and the precife time and manner of their taking place, will be fully known, and the prophecies by which they are foretold, will be better underftood, when they fhall be actually accomplifhed; and all the miftakes which are now made refpecting them, will be rectified ; until which time, they muft be in fome meafure fealed. Neverthelefs, it may be evident from divine revelation, that the end of the reign of antichrift draws near, and the time of deliverance of the church, from the dark and low ftate in which it has been near twelve hundred years, and of the ruin of the kingdom of fatan in the world, is not far off; and that thefe great events will come on within two hundred years, or about that time; and that the feventh thoufand years of the world, is the time fixed for the profperity of the church of Chrift, and the reign of the faints on earth. And it is hoped that what has been now obferved on this point, is fufficient to convince every unprejudiced, attentive inquirer, that there is fatisfactory evidence from prophecy, and other things contained in fcripture, that the predicted Millennium will take place at that time.

It has been obferved, that as antichrift rofe gradually, from one degree of influence and power to another, till he became a complete beaft, fo this perfecuting, idolatrous, antichriftian power will fall by degrees, until it is wholly taken out of the way : And there may, and probably will be, 1260 years between the moft remarkable fteps by which he rofe, and as great and remarkable fteps, by which he is to fall, and go into perdition.*

The

* The time of the captivity of the Jews by the Babylonians, was fixed in the prophecy of Jeremiah to feventy years. But this prediction had reference to different beginnings and endings. It was juft feventy years from the firft captivity, in the fourth year of Jehoiakim, when Daniel and many other Jews were carried to Babylon, to the decree of Cyrus, giving leave to the Jews to return, and ordering that the temple and Jerufalem fhould be rebuilt. And it was feventy years from the deftruction of Jerufalem and the temple, to the publifhing of the decree of Darius, by which the building of the temple was completed, and the Jews reftored to their former ftate.

So, the 1260 years of the captivity of the church of Chrift, in fpiritual Babylon, will doubtlefs have different beginnings, and confequently different endings. As the power and tyranny of the Bifhop and church of Rome

rofe

The corruption and apoftacy of the church had early beginnings, and the ufurped, tyrannical, and worldly power of the Bifhops, efpecially of the Bifhop of Rome, foon began to take place. The Apoftle Paul, fpeaking of the grand apoftacy which has actually taken place in the church of Rome, under the influence and power of the *man of fin,* that is, the Pope, fays, that the feeds of all this were then fown, and this myftery of iniquity did then begin to work with power and energy, ἐνερ γεῖται which was to be kept under powerful reftraints for a while, but fhould openly appear and be acted out when thefe reftraints fhould be taken off.* In the third century, " The Bifhops affumed, in many places, a princely authority, particularly thofe who had the greateft number of churches under their infpection, and who prefided over the moft oppulent affemblies. They appropriated to their evangelical function, the fplendid enfigns of temporal majefty : A throne furrounded with minifters, exalted above his equals the fervants of the meek and humble Jefus, and fumptuous garments dazzled the eyes and the minds of the multitude, into an ignorant veneration for their arrogated authority."† And about the middle of that century, Stephen, the Bifhop of Rome, a haughty, ambitious man, afpired to a fuperiority and power over all the other Bifhops and churches, and his preeminence in the church univerfal, was acknowledged. From this time, to the reformation from popery in the fixteenth century, when the Pope began to fall in a remarkable degree, and loft a great part of his power and influence, which he is never like to regain, are 1260 years. Luther, the firft reformer, arofe in the year of Chrift, 1517. If we reckon back from that time, 1260 years will carry us to the year 257, which is the very time in which Stephen, Bifhop of Rome, claimed and ufurped the power and preeminence abovementioned, and which was, in fome meafure at leaft, granted to him.

And as this man of fin, rofe higher and higher, and became more confpicuous by one remarkable ftep after another, in the fourth, fifth, fixth and feventh centuries, until he was publicly invefted with temporal dominion, about the middle of the eighth century,

rofe from lefs beginnings to their full height ; fo the fall is to be gradual, till it is completed : And from each remarkable advance, there are 1260 years, to as remarkable, fucceffive events, by which the kingdom and the power of the beaft fhall decline, and be utterly deftroyed.

* 2 Theff. ii. 3—8.
† Mofheim's Ecclefiaftical Hiftory : Third Century, Chap. II.

century, viz. in the year 756, when he became a complete beaft, and affumed the greateft authority, both in civil and religious matters, in the chriftian world, and in fact had more power and influence over all perfons and things in the church and ftate, than any other man; fo there is good reafon to conclude, he will gradually fall, by one remarkable event after another, from the time of the reformation in the fixteenth century, when his power and influence in the chriftian world were fo greatly eclipfed, until this fon of perdition fhall be utterly deftroyed, not far from the end of the twentieth century, or the beginning of the feventh thoufand years of the world. And with the fall of this fon of fatan, the kingdom of fatan, which has been fo great and ftrong in this world for fo long a time, will come to an end, and he will be caft out of the earth, and chained down in the bottomlefs pit : Which event will be fucceeded by the kingdom of heaven, which fhall comprehend all the men then on earth, in which the faints fhall reign a thoufand years.

The facts and events which have taken place fince that time, efpecially in the prefent century, coincide with fuch a conclufion, and ferve to ftrengthen and confirm it. The Pope and the hierarchy of the church of Rome, are finking with a rapid defcent.—The kings and nations who once wandered after this beaft, and joined to fupport and exalt this antichriftian power, now pay little regard to him. They neither love nor fear him much, but are rather difpofed to pull him down and ftrip him of his riches and power. The diffolution of the fociety of the Jefuits, banifhing them, and confifcating their riches, who were a great fupport of that church and the Pope ; the kings taking from the Pope the power which he claimed, as his right, to nominate and appoint all the bifhops to vacant fees, and actually taking it upon themfelves to do this, by which a vaft ftream of money which ufed to be poured into the coffers of the Pope, is taken from him, and falls into the hands of thefe kings :—The increafe and fpread of light, by which the tyranny, fuperftition and idolatry of the church of Rome and its hierarchy are more clearly difcerned, and expofed to the abhorence and contempt of men ; and efpecially the great increafe of the knowledge of the nature, reafonablenefs and importance of religious and civil liberty, and the rapid fpread of zeal among the nations to promote thefe : All thefe are remarkable events, which, among others not mentioned, ferve to

N                                                  confirm

confirm the above conclusion, that the Pope is falling with increasing rapidity. And there is reason to expect from what has come to pass, and is now taking place, and from scripture prophecy, that yet greater and more remarkable events will soon take place, and come on in a swift and surprising succession, which will hasten on the utter overthrow of the beast and all his adherents : And that the time predicted will soon come, when the ten horns, or kings, who have agreed in time past, and given their kingdom unto the beast, shall change their minds, and hate the whore, and make her desolate, and naked, and shall eat her flesh, and burn her with fire.*

* Rev. xvii. 16, 17.

# SECTION IV.

*In which is considered, what events are to take place, according to Scripture Prophecy, before the beginning of the Millennium, and to prepare the way for it.*

B Y attending to the events predicted, which are to take place before the Millennium, and which are to introduce it, farther evidence will come into view, that it will not commence long before the beginning of the seventh thousand years of the world ; nor much latter ; and. therefore, that it will be in that thousand years, and begin about two hundred years from the end of this present century.

The seven vials or cups, which contained the seven last plagues, or remarkable judgments, which are to be executed upon the beast and his adherents, and upon the world of mankind, are to be poured out during the time of the reign of the beast, and the existence of the false church of Rome ; and which will issue in the destruction of the beast, and of that church. This is evident from the fifteenth and sixteenth chapters of the Revelation. The first vial respects the beast and his followers, and brought sore calamities upon them, expressed in the following words : " And

there

there fell a noifome and grievous fore upon the men which had the mark of the beaft, and upon them who worfhipped his image."* A number of thefe vials muft have been already poured out, as the beaft has exifted above a thoufand years already ; and therefore the effects of the laft vial, which include his utter deftruction, will not reach much more than two hundred years from this time ; and confequently thefe effects will foon begin to take place, if they have not already began in fome meafure. For as the pouring out or running, of the feven vials, is limited to the 1260 years of the continuance of the beaft, there are not 200 years for each vial ; and fome may run longer, and others a fhorter time of this fpace.

Some acquaintance with the hiftory of the calamitous events which have taken place, anfwering to the prophetic defcription under thofe vials which have been poured out, is neceffary in order to know how and when it has been fulfilled, and how many vials appear to have already run out, and which is now running.— Mr. Lowman has taken pains to fhow from many credible hiftorians, that the remarkable calamitous events which have taken place, and which have efpecially affected the beaft and his followers, and brought great and diftreffing evils upon them, have anfwered to the evils and events defcribed in prophetic language, under the fucceffive five firft vials of wrath : And there appears to be fatisfactory evidence that the judgments predicted under thefe vials, have already been executed on antichrift, and his fupporters and followers : And that the reformation began by Luther, and the remarkable events attending it, was the judgment predicted by the pouring out of the fifth vial, to be inflicted on the beaft and the church of Rome. This vial was to be poured out on the feat, or, as it is in the original, the throne of the beaft—" And his kingdom was full of darknefs, and they gnawed their tongues for pain."† When the proteftant reformation came on, proteftants had light, had difcerning and wifdom, profperity and joy : But the Pope and his followers fuffered great vexation and anguifh, every event turned againft them, their light was turned into darknefs, their policy and counfels, by which they had profpered and obtained their ends before, were now turned into foolifhnefs ; and they were baffled and confounded, and their attempts to fupprefs the northern herefy, as they called it, and to crufh the proteftants, proved abortive, and turned againft themfelves, in a remarkable

N 2                                        manner.

* Rev. xvi. 2.          † Rev. xvi. 10.

manner.   And thofe events proved like a lafting, painful fore to them, from which they have not recovered to this day.   "And they blafphemed the God of heaven, becaufe of their pains and their fores, and repented not of their deeds."   They blafphemed God, by attributing what took place in favour of truth and the caufe of Chrift, to the exertions and obftinacy of wicked men, and calling the truths of the gofpel and holinefs, efpoufed and propagated by the reformers, the delufions and works of fatan, and treating the reformation, and the work of God, as if it were the work of the devil.   They alfo blafphemed the God of heaven, by perfifting in their grofs idolatry, worfhipping faints and images, in the face of the light exhibited by the reformers, which idolatry is called blafphemy in the Bible.   And the famous council of Trent, which was called by the Pope at that time, and fat eighteen years, were fo far from complying with the reformation, that they anathematized the perfons, doctrines and practices, by which it was introduced and fupported.   And formed decrees in favour of the power and tyranny of the Pope, and the fuperftition and idolatry of the church of Rome, and in fome inftances went beyond any thing that had ever been decreed by any counfel before, in favour of thefe abominations.   Thus "they repented not of their evil deeds."

This vial began to be poured out near the beginning of the fixteenth century, in the year 1517, when Luther began to oppofe the wickednefs of the church of Rome, and the power and evil practices of the Pope : And from that time, the influence and power, or throne, of this man of fin, has been diminifhing, and he is in a great meafure depofed,  and has fallen almoft to the ground from that high throne, and unlimited power in church and ftate, to which he had,  before that, afpired and rifen.   As it is near three hundred years fince the fifth vial was  poured out, there is good reafon to conclude, that the fixth vial began to be poured out, and has been running from the latter end of the laft century, at leaft, i. e. for an hundred years  or more ;  that it is near run out, and the feventh and laft vial will begin to run early in the next century.   Whether this be fo or not, may be determined with greater and more fatisfactory evidence, by attending to the prophetic defcription of the events which are to take place under thofe vials.   And as the fixth vial is fuppofed to be now running, there is reafon to pay a more particular and careful attention to

the

the prophetic language, by which the events under this vial are expreſſed, that the meaning may be underſtood, and applied to the events which are pointed out, ſo as to be clearly diſcovered, and the ſigns of theſe times, be diſcerned by all who will properly attend to this intereſting ſubject.

"And the ſixth angel poured out his vial upon the great river Euphrates : And the water thereof was dried up, that the way of the kings of the eaſt might be prepared." Ancient Babylon was a type of the antichriſtian church of Rome. By that, the church of Iſrael was afflicted and reduced to a ſtate of captivity ſeventy years, until it was taken by Cyrus and Darius, whoſe kingdoms were eaſt of Babylon. So the church of Chriſt has fallen under the power of this antichriſtian church, and power is given to the beaſt to make war with the ſaints, and to overcome them, and to continue forty two months : Therefore, the church of Rome is called Babylon in the Revelation.

The river Euphrates ran through Babylon, under the walls of the city, and a wide and deep moat, filled with water from the river, encompaſſed the city on the outſide of the walls ; ſo that the river was not only a defence to the city, but afforded a ſupply of water and fiſh, and other proviſions, brought into it by water carriage. Cyrus, who came againſt Babylon with an army of Medes and Perſians, took the city, by turning the water of the river from the uſual channel, in which it went under the walls of the city, and ran through it, and dried up the water in that chan- nel, by which a way was opened for his army to paſs into the city under the walls, in the dried channel, where the river uſed to run. Accordingly the army marched in, and took the city in the night, when the inhabitants were either aſleep, or intoxicated with drinking, as that was the time of a great feſtival. In that night the king of Babylon was ſlain, and Cyrus took the kingdom for his uncle Darius, the Mede.*

In this prophecy there is an alluſion to this manner of taking Babylon, by Darius and Cyrus, the kings of the eaſt. The church of Rome is the antitype of Babylon. By the kings of the eaſt, are meant thoſe, whoever they may be, who are, or ſhall be enemies to the church of Rome, and wiſh to reduce and deſtroy it, and ſhall be made the inſtruments of it ; as the eaſtern kings took Babylon, by drying up the river Euphrates. The riches and power of the

Pope

* Dan. v.——See Prideaux's Connexion, Part I Book II.

Pope and the church of Rome, and whatever serves as a defence
and support of that church, answer to the river Euphrates in old
Babylon; and the removal of those is meant by drying up the
river; which will prepare the way for the enemies and opposers
of this church, to take possession of it, and destroy it.

The river, in this sense of it, has been drying up for a century
or more, while this sixth vial has been running; and there have
been more remarkable instances of it in this century, some of which
have been mentioned above, by which the riches of the church of
Rome are greatly diminished, and she is stripped and becoming
poor: And the power and influence of the Pope is become very
small and inconsiderable, and he is but little regarded by those who
once worshipped him; and the way is fast preparing, for the
Pope and his church to be hated, made desolate, and burnt with
fire."*

John goes on to relate a farther vision which he had, of events
which are to take place under this vial, in the following words:
And I saw three unclean spirits like frogs come out of the mouth
of the dragon, and out of the mouth of the beast, and out of the
mouth of the false prophet. For they are the spirits of devils,
working miracles, which go forth unto the kings of the earth, and
of the whole world, to gather them to the battle of that great day
of God Almighty. And he gathered them together into a place,
called in the Hebrew tongue, Armageddon."† This is the first
time that the false prophet is mentioned: And it appears from
what is said of this false prophet, in the twentieth verse of the
nineteenth chapter, that he is the same with the second beast,
which is described in the thirteenth chapter, by which is meant
the hierarchy of the church of Rome, or the Pope and his clergy,
in their ecclesiastical capacity, claiming to have the sole jurisdiction,
and to be infalible dictators in every thing that relates to christian
faith and practice. The beast, as distinguished from the false
prophet here, is the civil power of the Roman empire, with which
the Pope is invested, which he has claimed and exercised, by which
he became a beast.

The dragon is the devil, who is represented as a powerful, invisible agent, having a great hand in all the wickedness in the
world, and has set up and animates the beast and false prophet,

making

* See Edward's Humble Attempt, &c. page 153.
† Rev. xvi. 13, 14, 16.

making them inftruments to anfwer his ends, being the fpirit who works with all his power and deceptive cunning, in thefe children of difobedience; and who are his children in a peculiar fenfe. Thefe fpirits are therefore, the numerous fpirits of devils who unite in one defign, working miracles, or wonders, as the word in the original is fometimes rendered, which go forth unto the kings of the earth, and of the whole world; that is, to all men who dwell on the earth, great and fmall, high and low. What is the tendency and effect of thefe invifible, evil fpirits, what they defign and do accomplifh, when thus let loofe, and fuffered to go forth into all the world, there can be no doubt. They will corrupt the world, and promote all kinds of wickednefs among men, to the utmoft of their power and fkill, and excite mankind to rife againft God and the Redeemer, and oppofe and defpife all divine inftitutions and commands; and, at the fame time, to hate and deftroy each other, and attempt to gratify every hateful luft of the flefh and of the mind, without reftraint.

If any diftinction is to be made between thofe evil fpirits which are united in the fame defign, and like frogs pervade all places and affault all men, as the frogs did the Egyptians, in their attempts to feduce and corrupt them; efpecially thofe who live in the chriftian world; that which comes out of the mouth of the dragon, promotes infidelity, and influences and perfuades men to renounce all religion; efpecially that which is inculcated in the Bible. The fpirit which proceeds from the mouth of the beaft, infpires men with a worldly fpirit, by which they are ftrongly attached to the things and enjoyments of this world, and eagerly purfue them; either by gratifying their flefhly appetites and lufts, in beaftly uncleannefs, and intemperance in eating and drinking, frolick and wantonnefs; or by indulging an avaricious fpirit, which leads to all kinds of unrighteoufnefs, and oppreffion of each other, according to their power and opportunity: Or they eagerly purfue the honours of the world, in the gratification of pride and haughtinefs, ftriving to outfhine others in drefs and high living, or in diftinguifhed pofts of honour. And though fome perfons under the influence of the fpirit of the beaft, are more inclined to fome one of thefe, and others to another; yet the fame perfon will often purfue them all, and feek to gratify the luft of the flefh, the luft of the eyes, and the pride of life. And all thefe will prevail more and more, under the influence of the fpirit of the beaft;

beaft ; and at the fame time promote infidelity, and are promoted by that. The fpirit which comes out of the mouth of the falfe prophet, is a fpirit of falfe religion and delufion, by which falfe doctrines and grofs errors in principle and practice, are imbibed and propagated.

Thefe fpirits of devils unite and are agreed in one defign, to promote all kind of vice and wickednefs among men, and to as great a degree as they poffibly can, leading them to infidelity and impiety, and an endlefs train of grofs errors and delufions, in matters of religion ; and hurrying them on in a greedy purfuit of the enjoyments of this world, in the indulgence of their lufts, and the gratification of their love of their own felves, and their pride, in the practice of injuftice and oppreffion, living in malice and envy, hating and fpeaking evil of one another, and engaging in fierce contention, cruel and deftructive war, and murder. By this the world in general, will be in arms againft God, and his Son ; and they will be gathered and knit together, as one man, in open war with heaven, and all the friends of Chrift on earth. This is doubtlefs meant by thefe fpirits of devils, going out into the whole world, to gather them to the battle of that great day of God Almighty. It is not meant, that they fhall be gathered into one place on this globe, or any where alfe ; but that they fhall be united with one heart in the fame caufe of fin and fatan, againft God, and his revealed truth and ways, in whatever part of the earth they live ; and thus take arms, and rife in open rebellion, provoking the Almighty to battle, and, in a fenfe, challenging him to do his worft.—— Thus they will be as really gathered to the battle, as an army are gathered together to engage in battle with another army, or to befiege a city.

" And he gathered them together into a place called in the Hebrew tongue Armageddon." Armageddon is the mountain of Megiddo, at the foot of which the memorable battle was fought between the Canaanites, the enemies of Ifrael—and Barak, and the army under him, when Sifera and his hoft were defeated and utterly deftroyed ; which was a complete overthrow of the Canaanites, and iffued in the final deliverance of Ifrael from their yoke and power. This was a type of the total defeat and overthrow of the enemies of Chrift and his church, which will iffue in the peace and profperity of the church in the Millennium ftate. This is intimated in the concluding words of the fong of Deborah

and

and Barak, in which this victory and deliverance is celebrated.
" So let all thine enemies perish, O Lord : But let them who love
him, be as the sun when he goeth forth in his might."* There
is therefore an allusion to the type, in this prophecy of the event
which was typified by it, viz.—the overthrow of all the combined
enemies of Christ and his church, in the battle of that great day of
God Almighty. It cannot be reasonably inferred from this prediction, that there will be a decisive battle between Christ and his
followers, and their enemies, in any particular place. All that is
signified by these words is, that as Jabin king of Canaan gathered
together a great army under Sisera, to fight with the God of
Israel and his people, at the foot of the mountain of Megiddo ;
who were there overthrown and destroyed in battle, when " they
fought from heaven, the stars in their courses fought against Sisera :" So by the agency of the spirits of devils, under the super-
intendence and direction of divine providence, the world of mankind in general, and especially those in Christendom, will be so
corrupted and obstinately rebellious, in all kinds, and the greatest
degrees of wickedness, as to be united, and, in this sense, gathered
together, all armed in a spiritual war against God, his cause and
people. And their iniquity being full, and they ripe for the battle,
God will arise as a man of war, and in his providence contend in
battle with them, till they be utterly destroyed from the face of
the earth. Thus " The wicked shall perish, and the enemies of
the Lord shall be as the fat of lambs, they shall consume : Into
smoke shall they consume away," and by this, way shall be made
for the meek to inherit the earth, and delight themselves in the
abundance of peace.†

But this battle is to come on under the next vial, which is the
seventh and last. When mankind shall be prepared and gathered
together, by the great degree of all kinds of wickedness, while
God has been waiting upon them, even to long suffering, in the
use of very powerful, and all proper means to reclaim and reform
them, he will arise to battle, and by doing terrible things in righteousness, will manifest and display his awful displeasure with
them, for their great wickedness, and obstinacy in rebellion against
him ; and the events will then take place which are predicted under the seventh vial.

" And the seventh angel poured out his vial into the air : And
there came a great voice out of the temple of heaven, from the

O                                              throne,

* Judg. v. 31.            † Psal. xxxvii. 11, 20.

throne, saying, IT IS DONE." This vial being poured out into the air, denotes that it should affect and destroy satan's kingdom, and his followers in the world in general, who is the prince of the power of the AIR. And the voice from heaven, saying, *It is done*, is a prediction that the events under this vial, by which the battle before mentioned is to be carried on and completed, will utterly destroy the interest and kingdom of the devil in the world, and finish the awful scene of divine judgments, on the antichristian church, and the wicked world in general. The prophecy then goes on to give a general and summary account of the battle of that great day, from the seventh verse to the end of the chapter, and the great and marvellous effects it will have upon great Babylon, i. e. the church of Rome, and upon the nations of the world in general. There will be the greatest convulsions and revolutions in the political and moral world, that have ever been, attended with awful judgments upon men ; which are predicted in prophetic language, " And there were voices, and thunders, and lightnings, and a great earthquake, such as was not since men were upon the earth, so mighty an earthquake, and so great. And every island fled away, and the mountains were not found."— " And the great city was divided into three parts, and the cities of the nations fell : And great Babylon came into remembrance before God, to give unto her the cup of the wine of the fierceness of his wrath." The great city, and great Babylon, seem to be one and the same thing, the church of Rome. In the next chapter, this same false church is called " Babylon the great," and " The great city which reigneth over the kings of the earth."* What is meant by this city being divided into three parts will be better known, when the prediction shall be accomplished. It doubtless intends, that which shall break the antichristian church into pieces, and will issue in the ruin of it, the fatal blow being struck. Perhaps it intends a division and opposition among those who have been the members and supporters of that church, by which this spiritual Babylon shall fall, or which shall hasten on the ruin of it ; as a kingdom divided against itself, cannot stand, but is brought to desolation. In the prophecy of this kingdom of antichrist by Daniel, in the latter end of it, he says, " The kingdom shall be *divided* ; and by this it shall be partly broken.†

" And the cities of the nations fell." Divine judgments, and a peculiar measure of wrath shall fall upon the christian world, in

which

* Verses 5, 18. † Dan. ii. 41, 42.

which the antichriftian kingdom has been fet up ; but the reft of mankind fhall fhare in the calamity of that day, and be punifhed for their wickednefs, to which this expreffion feems to have refpect. The cities of the nations of the world, are their ftrength, defence and pride : Thefe fhall be demolifhed and wholly taken away, that they fhall no more be able to tyrannize over one another.—— The pride and power of Mahometans and heathen nations, fhall be made to ceafe by a feries of divine judgments.  " The day of the Lord of hofts fhall be upon every one that is proud and lofty, and upon every one that is lifted up, and he fhall be brought low. And upon every high tower, and upon every fenced wall.  And the loftinefs of man fhall be bowed down, and the haughtinefs of men fhall be made low, in that day.   And I will punifh the world for their evil, and the wicked for their iniquity ; and I will caufe the arrogancy of the proud to ceafe, and will lay low the haughti- nefs of the terrible."*   The fame is predicted in the following words : "I have cut off the nations, their towers are defolate; I have made their ftreets wafte, that none paffeth by : *Their cities are deftroyed*, fo that there is no man, there is none inhabitant.   There- fore wait upon me, faith the Lord, until the day that I rife up to the prey : For my determination is to gather the nations, that I may affemble the kingdoms to pour upon them mine indignation, even all my fierce anger ; for the earth fhall be devoured with the fire of my jealoufy."†   Thefe words doubtlefs have reference to the events which were to take place under the fixth and feventh vials, when the nations and kingdoms of the world are to be *gathered*, and God will rife up to battle, to the prey, and pour upon them his indignation, even all his fierce anger, for their obftinate continuance in fin and rebellion againft him ; and all the earth fhall be devoured with the fire of his jealoufy ; and thus the cities of the nations fhall fall ; the nations fhall be cut off ; their towers made defolate, and their cities deftroyed.

The prophecy under the feventh vial goes on.   " And there fell upon men a great hail out of heaven, every ftone about the weight of a talent : And men blafphemed God, becaufe of the plague of the hail ; for the plague thereof was exceeding great." There is reference in thofe words to the deftruction of the Cana- anites, in the great and terrible battle, when the Lord caft down great ftones from heaven upon them, and they died, and there

were

* Ifai. ii. 12, 13, 17. xiii. 11.         † Zeph. iii. 6, 8

were more that died with hailſtones, than they whom the children of Iſrael ſlew with the ſword.* And God ſays to Job, " Haſt thou ſeen the treaſures of hail, which I have reſerved againſt the time of trouble, againſt *the day of battle and war·"*† Therefore, when great judgments and awful deſtruction of men are predicted, they are repreſented by ſtorms of great hail. " Behold, the Lord hath a mighty and ſtrong one, which as a tempeſt of hail, and a deſtroy- ing ſtorm, ſhall caſt down to the earth with the hand. Judgment alſo will I lay to the line, and righteouſneſs to the plummet, and the hail ſhall ſweep away the refuge of lies. The Lord ſhall cauſe his glorious voice to be heard, and ſhall ſhew the lighting down of his arm, with the indignation of his anger, and with the flame of devouring fire, with ſcattering and tempeſt and hail- ſtones."‡ " Say unto them who daub with untempered mortar, that it ſhall fall : There ſhall be an overflowing ſhower, and ye, O great hailſtones, ſhall fall, and a ſtormy wind ſhall rent it. I will even rent it with a ſtormy wind in my fury : And there ſhall be an overflowing ſhower in mine anger, and great hailſtones in my fury to comſume it. And I will plead againſt him with peſti- lence, and with blood, and I will rain upon him, and his bands, and upon many people that are with him, an overflowing rain, and great hailſtones, fire and brimſtone."§ All theſe paſſages‖ will doubtleſs have their ultimate and moſt complete fulfilment, under the ſeventh vial, and in the ſame ſore calamities and judgments which are predicted in the words under conſideration, by the great hail which fell on men out of heaven. The hailſtones are repre- ſented as weighing an hundred pounds, which is the weight of a talent, to denote the greatneſs of the judgments and deſtruction predicted, the ſore and awful diſtreſſes which ſhall come on men : " For the plague thereof was exceeding great." Theſe judg- ments will not reform the obſtinate enemies of God, on whom

they

---

* Joſh. x. 11. † Job xxxviii. 22, 23.

‡ Iſai. xxviii. 2, 17. xxx. 30. § Ezek. xiii. 11, 13. xxxviii. 22.

‖ Unleſs that in Ezekiel be an exception, which is a deſcription of the puniſhment of Gog and Magog, by which name the multitude of wicked men are called, who ſhall riſe up when the Millennium is ended, and will be deſtroyed when Chriſt ſhall come to judgment. Theſe words may have their *ultimate* accompliſhment then. But as the Gog and Magog of Ezekiel repreſent the wicked world which ſhall be deſtroyed before the Millennium begins, as well as thoſe who ſhall riſe up when it will end ; this paſſage has a primary, if not an ultimate reference to the deſtruction of the former.

they shall fall; they will be exasperated and blaspheme God, the more, until they are utterly destroyed, and swept off from the earth; agreeably to the prophecy which may be considered as refering ultimately to this dreadful scene. " And they shall pass through it, hardly bestead and hungry : And it shall come to pass, that when they shall be hungry, they shall fret themselves, and curse their king and their God, and look upward. And they shall look unto the earth; and behold, trouble and darkness, dimness of anguish; and they shall be driven into darkness."*

This battle is more particularly described in the nineteenth chapter, from the beginning of the eleventh verse, to the end of the chapter. " And I saw heaven opened, and beheld, a white horse; and he who sat upon him was called faithful and true, and in righteousness doth he judge and make war." This person is farther described, by which he appears to be the Lord Jesus Christ. " And the armies which were in heaven, followed him upon white horses, clothed in fine linen, white and clean." This does not mean, that the inhabitants of heaven, or the saints on earth, will join in a visible army, and personally fight with the enemies of Christ and his church, and destroy them : But only that these shall join with Christ and be on his side, when he shall arise in his providence, and by his power destroy his and their enemies. In this sense, all heaven will be with him, when he shall come forth to battle in his providence, and execute his wrath upon men, in awful successive judgments, in which the angels may be used as invisible instruments of his vengeance : And he will do all this, in answer to the prayers of his church on earth, and in their cause, to vindicate and deliver them, and prepare the way for the prosperity of his church on earth. That he will be the great invisible agent in this battle, appears from the following words : And out of his mouth goeth a sharp sword, that with it he should smite the nations : And he shall rule them with a rod of iron : And he treadeth the wine press of the fierceness and wrath of Almighty God." This is the battle of that great day of God Almighty. This awful scene proceeds and is yet farther described : " And I saw an angel standing in the sun; and he cried with a loud voice, saying to all the fowls that fly in the midst of heaven, Come and gather yourselves together unto the supper of the great God; that ye may eat the flesh of kings, and the

flesh

flesh of captains, and the flesh of mighty men, and the flesh of horses, and of them that fit on them, and the flesh of all men, both small and great." This is a strong, figurative, prophetic expression of the great slaughter and terrible destruction of mankind, when God Almighty shall come forth to battle, and manifest his hot displeasure and terrible wrath, in the judgment he will inflict on them. The representation of this battle, and the issue of it goes on, and " I John saw the beast, and the kings of the earth, and their armies *gathered together*, to make war against him who sat on the horse, and against his army." These are the same who are mentioned, chap. xvi. 14, 16, as *gathered together* to the battle of that great day of God Almighty, the meaning of which has been explained. And in this war and battle, the beast and the false prophet were taken and destroyed, with their adherents. " And the remnant were slain with the sword of him who sat upon the horse, which sword proceedeth out of his mouth, and all the fowls were filled with their flesh." By *the remnant*, are meant the rest of mankind, who by their sins make war with Christ, and are not included in the beast and false prophet, and their followers, who belong to the kingdom of antichrist. Their being slain by the sword which proceeded out of the mouth of Christ, does not mean their conversion, but their falling victims to his vengeance, which is expressed by the fowls being filled with their flesh.

The same battle and slaughter of men, is represented and predicted in figurative prophetic language, in the fourteenth chapter, where John describes a vision which he had of one like unto the Son of man, who sat upon a white cloud, having on his head a golden crown, and in his hand a sharp sickle. And it was said unto him, " Thrust in thy sickle and reap ; for the time is come for thee to reap ; for the harvest of the earth is ripe. And he thrust in his sickle on the earth, and the earth was reaped. And another angel came out of the temple which is in heaven, he also having a sharp sickle." And it was said unto him, Thrust in thy sharp sickle, and gather the clusters of the vine of the earth ; for her grapes are fully ripe. And the angel thrust in his sickle into the earth, and gathered the vine of the earth, and cast it into the great wine press of the wrath of God. And the wine press was trodden without the city, and blood came out of the wine press, even unto the horse bridles, by the space of a thousand and six hundred furlongs."

Upon this vision it is to be observed, that by the harveft of the earth, and the clusters of the vine of the earth, are meant the inhabitants of the earth, or mankind in general. And reaping the harveft, and gathering the clusters of the vine of the earth, fignifies the slaughter and deftruction of the inhabitants of the earth; not every one of them indeed; for in the harveft and vintage, fome ears of corn are commonly left ftanding, which escape the fickle, and a few fcattering grapes are left on the vine when the clusters in general are gathered: And that this slaughter and defolation, which fhall be made of the inhabitants of the world, will take place in confequence of their apoftacy, and obftinate continuance and increafe in fin, until they are become ripe, fully ripe, for this dreadful execution and deftruction, by divine vengeance: Therefore, that this reaping, and the harveft, and gathering the clusters of the vine of the earth, will not be a merciful difpenfation towards the inhabitants then in the world; but the execution of divine vengeance, and an awful exercife and difplay of the difpleafure and wrath of God, in the evils which fhall fall on men, for their perfeverance and increafe in wickednefs. This is reprefented and exprefled in a ftriking manner, by the figure of cafting the vintage into the great wine prefs of the wrath of God, and the large and amazing quantity of blood which proceeded from thence; fignifying the great and general slaughter, and terrible fufferings of mankind, when this time of his wrath fhall come.

From this view of the events predicted under the fixth and feventh vials, it appears, that while the fixth vial is running, the way will be preparing for the overthrow of fpiritual Babylon.

One event will take place after another, which will greatly weaken and remove the power and influence of the Pope, among the nations in Chriftendom, by taking away his riches, by drying up the ftream of wealth, and the removal of other things, by which the church of Rome has been made ftrong, and ftood as impregnable for many ages. But this will not be attended by any general reformation of profeffing chriftians, or revival and great increafe of the true church of Chrift; nor will the moral ftate of the chriftian world, or of mankind in general, be reformed and grow better, but the contrary. By the evil influence which the beaft and the hierarchy of the church of Rome, has had in the world, and by the power and agency of fatan, the unreftrained lufts of men will hurry them on to all kinds of wickednefs; fo that it will rife to a

greater

greater degree, and be more univerfal than ever before. Infidelity, deifm, and atheifm, and the moft open and grofs impiety and profanation of every thing facred, will prevail and abound. And falfe religion, and the groffeft errors and delufions of all kinds, will take place and fpread among thofe who do not difcard all religion. And a worldly fpirit will be very ftrong and prevalent, among old and young, urging them on to the gratification of their fenfual inclinations and lufts, in all kinds of intemperance and lewdnefs; and prompting them to acts of unrighteoufnefs, oppreffion and cruelty; which will promote mutual hatred, bitternefs and contention, and fpread confufion, and every evil work, in fierce and cruel wars, and horrid murders. It is certain, that the unclean fpirits, like frogs, thofe fpirits of devils, when they go forth to the whole world, will promote all kinds of diforder and wickednefs to the greateft degree, and fet mankind againft God, and all his revealed truth, and againft each other, and every thing good and excellent; and make this world as much an image of hell as they poffibly can; by which the inhabitants on earth, in general, will be united and gathered together in arms againft heaven, and become wholly ripe for deftruction from the Almighty, for the battle of that great day, which will come on under the feventh vial, and will be conducted, fought and finifhed by Chrift himfelf, againft an ungodly world.

The prevailing, unreftrained wickednefs of men, which has been now mentioned, by which they fhall be gathered unto this battle, is defcribed by the Apoftle Paul, in the following words: " This know alfo, that in the laft days, perilous times fhall come. For men fhall be lovers of their ownfelves, covetous, boafters, proud, blafphemers, difobedient to parents, unthankful, unholy, without natural affection, covenant breakers, falfe accufers, incontinent, fierce, defpifers of thofe who are good, traitors, heady, highminded, lovers of pleafures more than lovers of God; having a form of godlinefs, but denying the power thereof."* All thefe evil characters have been in every age of the world; but they will then, in thefe *laft days*, take place to a greater degree, and more univerfally, than ever before.

The true church of Chrift will fubfift and continue in this evil time of the prevalence of the powers of darknefs; but the number of real chriftians will be fmall; and many, even of them, if not

the

* 2 Tim. iii. 1, 2, 3, 4, 5.

the moft, will probably be weak and low in their chriftian exercifes, by the influences and uncommon power of thofe evil fpirits, and in too great a degree conformed to this world. They will be hated, oppofed, and trodden down, by the wicked, and be in an afflicted, fuffering ftate in this dark and evil day. They will be in a great meafure hidden and unknown, and the caufe of Chrift and of truth will be reproached, and appear to be almoft loft ; and the true followers of Chrift, his fheep, will be fcattered into corners in this cloudy and dark day.* Whether wicked men, and enemies to the true fervants of Chrift, will perfecute them unto death, and renew this horrid work, of which fo much has been done in former ages, in this time when iniquity will abound to fuch a great degree, cannot be now determined, by any thing faid in fcripture refpecting it. It is thought by moft, that fince the Pope is brought fo low, and his power and influence is ftill finking fo faft ; and fo much light is fpreading in favour of civil and religious liberty, fhowing the reafonablenefs and importance of it, and the unreafonablenefs and folly of a perfecuting fpirit ; and liberal fentiments refpecting religion are propagated and increafing, perfecution on account of religious fentiments or practice, is near come to an end, and never will be revived and practifed again.—— This may appear moft probable : But though the antichriftian church fhould never perfecute the faithful followers of Chrift again, and a perfecuting fpirit fhould wholly ceafe among profeffing chriftians of all denominations ; yet infidels, who condemn all religious perfecution, in every degree and form, in which it has been practifed, and boaft of their liberal fentiments and fpirit, with refpect to this ; and ufe it as a ftrong and conclufive argument againft chriftianity itfelf, that profeffed chriftians have, in fo many inftances, perfecuted others ; even *thefe infidels,* or their fucceffors, may find true chriftians, their doctrines and practices, to be fo difagreeable and hateful to them, and, in their view, fo hurtful to fociety, and fo contrary to all that, in which they place their own happinefs, and that of mankind, that having all reftraints taken off, and the power being put into their hands, they may think thefe men ought not to be fuffered to live ; and that it is for the good of fociety to have them extirpated, and put to death, unlefs they can be brought to renounce their fentiments and practices, by perfuafion or punifhments ; and fo become as determined,

P                                                    cruel

* Ezek. xxxiv. 12.

cruel perfecutors of chriftians, as any have been in paft ages.——
If this fhould take place, it will make a new, and perhaps greater
and more ftriking difcovery of the wickednefs of the human heart,
efpecially of the hearts and real character of this fort of men, than
ever has been exhibited before. And they who now know what
is in man, from the character given of him in fcripture, and by
the difcovery mankind have made of their hearts, by words and
deeds, and from a true acquaintance with their own hearts, muft
be fenfible that nothing can prevent even men of this caft perfecuting chriftians, but reftraints from heaven. But, however, perhaps
this difcovery of what is in man, is referved to be made after the
Millennium fhall be over, in the rife of Gog and Magog, when it
may be exhibited, in many refpects, to greater advantage, and fo
as to anfwer more important ends.

Though the true church of Chrift muft be in a low, dark ftate,
in many refpects, under this vial, yet there will doubtlefs be revivals of religion, and an increafe of converts to real chriftianity, in
many different places, and truth may be getting advantage, and
more clearly diftinguifhed from error, by thofe who have eyes to
fee ; and chriftianity be more and more refined in doctrines and
practice, from the various errors and corruptions, which have been
introduced among the true followers of Chrift ; and every thing,
and all events, will ferve to bring on and introduce the Millennium,
in the beft manner, and in the moft proper time.

The battle of that great day of God Almighty, is to come on
under the feventh vial, as has been obferved. When the iniquity
of the world of mankind fhall be full, and they fhall be united in
open rebellion, and, in this fenfe, gathered together, and armed
againft heaven : And after God has waited long upon them in
the ufe of all proper means to reclaim them, efpecially the chriftian
world ; and they are become fully ripe for deftruction, he will
come forth to battle againft them, and execute moft fearful judgments upon them, and deftroy them in a manner and degree,
which fhall manifeft his awful difpleafure with them, for their
obftinacy in all kinds of wickednefs. When thefe briars and
thorns are fet againft God in battle, he will go through them
and burn them together.* The deftruction of the world of mankind by a flood, when the wickednefs of man was become great,
and the earth was filled with violence ; and they continued obftinate

in

* See Ifai. xxvii. 4.

in difobedience, while the long fuffering of God waited upon them in the days of Noah, was an emblem of this battle: As alfo was the deftruction of the inhabitants of Canaan, when their iniquity was full, which prepared the way for the people of God to take poffeffion of that land. So God punifhed the nation of the Jews, by deftroying them, and laying wafte Jerufalem, and the temple. When they had filled up the meafure of their fins, wrath came upon them to the uttermoft. This was a figure or type of this greater, more dreadful and general battle, under the feventh vial, when " The Lord fhall come out of his place to punifh the inhabitants of the earth for their iniquity, and the earth fhall difclofe her blood, and fhall no more cover her flain."\*

This battle, it has been obferved, will not confift in the church or chriftians raifing armies, and fighting and carrying on war with the antichriftian party, or with the wicked world ; or in a conflict between the former and the latter, refpecting the truths and caufe of Chrift : But it will be commenced and carried on by Chrift, while invifible in heaven, invefted with all divine power in heaven and earth, in the exercife of his providence, bringing judgments upon his enemies, and a wicked world, in fuch remarkable ways and manner, as to be a clear and remarkable manifeftation of his prefence and power ; of his difpleafure with a wicked world, for oppofing him, his church and the gofpel ; and an inconteftible evidence of the truth of chriftianity, by fulfilling his predictions and promifes, taking vengeance on the enemies of his people, and effectually fupporting them, and their caufe. He will doubtlefs make ufe of inftruments in this battle.

The holy angels may be made the inftruments of many events which fhall be full of evil to wicked men. And the true church of Chrift, his witneffes in his caufe, and againft the delufions and wickednefs of the antichriftian church, and of the world, are reprefented as having a hand in bringing upon their enemies all the evils which will come upon them ; becaufe they will take place in anfwer to their prayers, in their caufe, and in order effectually to avenge his own elect of their adverfaries.† Therefore, it is faid of them, " Thefe have power to fhut heaven, that it rain not, in the days of their prophecy : And have power over waters, to turn them into blood, and to fmite the earth with all plagues, as often as they will."‡ And the wicked themfelves will be inftru-

P 2                                                    ments

ments of afflicting and deftroying each other, in a very cruel and
dreadful manner, by oppofing and fighting with one another,
and carrying on deftructive and bloody wars, killing men by thoufands, and laying wafte whole countries and nations ; by which
the earth will be in a great degree depopulated ; and rivers of
blood will be fhed by the unreftrained pride and cruel rage of man.
And many will probably put an end to their own lives, and inftances of fuicide will be greatly multiplied.

But multitudes of mankind will be deftroyed by the more im-
mediate hand of God, by famine and peftilences, which will prevail
in many countries, at different times, in an extraordinary manner,
and to a degree never known before ; by which vaft multitudes
will perifh fuddenly, and in circumftances very furprifing and
awful.    And there will be earthquakes, and terrible ftorms of
lightning and thunder, and inundations of water, by which many
cities and places fhall fink and be overflowed, with all the inhabitants ; and multitudes will perifh by thefe, and innumerable other
evil occurrents, which will take place in an unufual manner, and
in quick fucceffion ; fo that the hand of God will be vifibly
ftretched out againft the inhabitants of the world, to punifh and
deftroy them for their wickednefs ; and the following prediction
will be fulfilled, in the full and awful extent of it.   "Fear, and
the pit, and the fnare, are upon thee, O inhabitant of the earth.
And it fhall come to pafs, that he who fleeth from the noife of the
fear, fhall fall into the pit ; and he that cometh up out of the
midft of the pit, fhall be taken in the fnare :  For the windows
from on high are open, and the foundations of the earth do fhake.
The earth is utterly broken down, the earth is clean diffolved,
the earth is moved exceedingly.   The earth fhall reel to and fro
like a drunkard, and fhall be removed like a cottage, and the tranfgreffion thereof fhall be heavy upon it, and it fhall fall, and not
rife again."*

This battle will not be fought at once, fo as to be foon finifhed ;
but will be carried on through a courfe of years, probably for more
than a century and an half, in order to make a fuitable and fufficiently clear difplay of the difpleafure of God with a wicked world ;
and to give opportunity to men to repent and reform, when they
are warned, called upon, and urged to it, by being made to fuffer fuch
a variety and long continued feries of calamities, for their fins ;

                                                                    and

* Ifai. xxiv. 17, 18, 19, 20.

and to difcover, and fet in the moſt clear and ſtriking light, the hardnefs, obſtinacy and wickednefs of the heart of man, while they continue difobedient and inflexible, under all thefe terrible difpenfations of providence, fuited to awaken and reform them, to teach them the evil of fin, and the awful difpleafure of God with them ; and to warn them to fly from the wrath to come, and unto Chriſt, as the only refuge; and go on to revolt yet more and more, and blafpheme the hand which inflicts thefe evils. By all this will be more clearly manifeſted, than ever before, how totally loſt and infinitely miferable mankind are, and their infinite need of a Redeemer ; that no means that can be ufed, or methods taken to reclaim and fave them, will be in the leaſt degree effectual, unlefs the Spirit of God be given to change and renew their hearts, and therefore, that the falvation of men depends wholly on the mere fovereign grace of God, even all that good, holinefs and falvation, which fhall take place in the Millennium ; and it will, in this refpect, prepare the way for that day of grace.

This battle and terrible ſlaughter and deſtruction of men in fo many ways, and for fo long a courfe of years, will greatly leffen the number of mankind in the world ; fo that in the clofe of this terrible fcene, comparatively few will be left alive. Thofe will be the chriſtians who fhall be then members of the churches, and defcendents from good people who have lived in former ages, and others who will then be true penitents, who will look back on the terrible fcene which had taken place in the battle of the great day of God Almighty, and fee, and have a clear and affecting conviction of his difpleafure with mankind, for their fins and the terriblenefs of his wrath ; and will acknowledge the righteoufnefs of it. They will confequently fee the guilty, miferable, and utterly loſt ſtate of man, and their need of a Redeemer, to make atonement for their fins, and the neceffity of the Holy Spirit to renew their hearts, and form them to right, and truly chriſtian exercifes : And will be clearly convinced of the truth of all the great and important doctrines of the gofpel, and cordially embrace them. And they will repent and humble themfelves in the fight of the Lord, and earneſtly, with united hearts, cry to heaven for the forgivenefs of their fins, and for mercy on themfelves, and on their children, acknowledging their infinite ill defert, and flying to Chriſt, and fovereign grace through him, as their only refuge and hope. And then the fcene will change. The battle will be over, divine

judgments

judgments will ceafe, and there will be no more frowns on man, in the providence of God; but all difpenfations and events will be expreffions of kindnefs and mercy; and the Holy Spirit will be poured out on them and their offspring, and all fhall be holinefs to the Lord; and the Millennium will begin, and men will multiply and foon fubdue the earth, and fill it with inhabitants.

As antichrift and the church of Rome, will have a large fhare in the cup of indignation and wrath which will be poured out; fo all the chriftian world will have a diftinguifhed portion of it, as the inhabitants of it are much more guilty than others. There is no reafon to confider the antichriftian fpirit and practices to be confined to that which is now called the church of Rome: The proteftant churches have much of antichrift in them, and are far from being wholly reformed from the corruptions and wickednefs, in doctrine and practice, which are found in that which is called BABYLON THE GREAT, THE MOTHER OF HARLOTS, AND A-BOMINATIONS OF THE EARTH. Her influence in promoting delufion and wickednefs extends, in fome degree, to all the inhabitants of the world, and more efpecially the chriftian world. She is the *Mother* of all the falfe doctrines, fuperftition, infidelity, and abominable practices in the proteftant world. And where can the church be found, which is thoroughly purged from all thefe abominations? Some churches may be more pure, and may have proceeded farther in a reformation than others; but none are wholly clear of an antichriftian fpirit, and the fruits of it. There may be, and in many inftances doubtlefs there is, much of the exercife of the fpirit of antichrift, in oppofing what is called antichrift, and the church of Rome; and by running into as great extremes another way. The Apoftle Paul faid, this myftery of iniquity, the man of fin, which is antichrift, began already to work in the churches even in his day.* How much of this then, may it be reafonably thought, is to be found in moft, if not all the churches now? In this view, the fpirit and operation of antichrift are very extenfive. And how few churches, or individual chriftians, have fo far come out from this mother of harlots, and abominations of the earth, as not to be in any degree partakers of her fins, fo as not to receive of her plagues? And while the fixth vial continues to run, it is not to be expected that the proteftant churches in general will grow more pure; but the evil fpirits which are gone forth, will

* 2 Theff. ii. 7.

will promote and fpread ftill greater corruption in doctrine and practice, by which they will be more ripe for divine judgments, and prepared to fuffer in the battle under the feventh vial. The pureft churches, and real chriftians, will fuffer much in this battle, and few will go wholly unpunifhed. By this the rebels, or falfe hearted profeffing chriftians, will be purged out from among real chriftians, and thefe fhall be purified and made white, and tried ; but the wicked fhall do wickedly.*

The Jews have fuffered greatly for their peculiarly aggravated wickednefs, in rejecting and crucifying the Son of God ; and they are now, and have been for near two thoufand years, in a ftate of great affliction, and under the manifeft difpleafure of heaven, to a great and diftinguifhed degree. They yet continue a people, dif-tinguifhed from all other nations, though fcatterrd all over the world, as outcafts and vagabonds ; and will continue thus a dif-tinct people down to the Millennium. But though they have fuf-fered fo much, they yet continue as obftinate as ever in rejecting Chrift, and in all their fins. And there is reafon to think they will not efcape the battle of the great day of Almighty God ; but great and new calamities will fall upon them, by which they may be much diminifhed, fo as to be left few in number, compared with what they have been, or are now. And the threatning denounced againft that people by Mofes, will then be executed on them, in the full meaning and extent of it : " And ye fhall be left few in number, whereas ye were as the ftars of heaven for multitude : Becaufe thou wouldeft not obey the voice of the Lord thy God."† But God will not make a full end of them, which he probably will do of fome, if not of many other nations.

The revolutions which will take place in this battle, will open the way for their return to the land given to their anceftors ; and they which are left will repent and return to the Lord Jefus Chrift, againft whom, they and their fathers have finned, and unto their own land, and will become an eminently excellent part of the chriftian church, who fhall multiply, and fill all that vaft tract of land given to Abraham and his pofterity, from the river of Egypt, to the great river Euphrates,‡ which has never yet been fully pof-feffed by them. And their being thus received into the church of Chrift, will be as life from the dead to them, and to the Gentiles.

But

* Dan. xii. 10.    † Deut. xxviii. 62.    ‡ Gen. xv. 18.

But whether they will continue a diftinct people from all other chriftians, through the whole time of the Millennium, or be fo intermixed with others, as not to be diftinguifhed from them, will be determined by the event : But the latter is moft probable, as the ends of their being preferved in fuch a ftate of diftinction, will then be anfwered ; and thofe circumftances and things, which have been, and ftill are, the means of their continuing a diftinct and feparate people, will then ceafe ; fuch as circumcifion, and their obfervance of other Mofaic rites. When they fhall become chriftians, their name by which they are now diftinguifhed will be loft, and they will be abforbed in the chriftian church, the true Ifrael of God, where there is neither Jew nor Greek, but all are one in Chrift : And then there will be one fold, and one fhepherd. And then, by this event, the following prediction will be fully accomplifhed : " And ye fhall leave your name for a curfe unto my chofen ! For the Lord God fhall flay thee, and call his fervants by another name."*

That the above reprefentation of this battle, which will be previous to the Millennium, and will introduce it, taken from the paffages in the Revelation which have been confidered, is juft, and agreeable to the true fenfe of them, farther appears, and is confirmed by other parts of holy fcripture, efpecially by the prophecies of this fame event, recorded in the Old Teftament.

The deftruction of the world of mankind by a flood, and the prefervation of Noah and his family, who were by this brought into a new world, to be replenifhed by them, may be confidered as a typical and prophetic reprefentation of the great battle with the wicked world, previous to the Millennium ; by which the wicked will be fwept off the earth, and the true church of Chrift will be delivered and preferved, and the way opened for its profperity, and filling the earth.

The feries of judgments brought upon Pharaoh and the Egyptians, for their difobedience to Jehovah, and oppreffions of his people, and their dreadful overthrow in the Red Sea, to prepare the way for the deliverance of Ifrael, was alfo a prophetic type of this great battle. So was the deftruction of the inhabitants of Canaan, in order to introduce the people of Ifrael, and put them in poffeffion of that land. Therefore, reference is had to this in the reprefentation of the battle of that great day, as has been obferved.

David

* Ifai. lxv. 15.

David was a man of blood, carried on great wars and deftroyed much people, and many nations, who were enemies to him, and the people of God ; and by his conquefts prepared the way for the peaceable and glorious reign of Solomon, and the building of the temple. In this, David was a type of Chrift, when he fhall go forth, clothed with a vefture dipt in blood, and in righteoufnefs make war, and deftroy the nations of mankind, his enemies, to prepare the way for the Millennium. Solomon was a type of Chrift reigning in the Millennium, when the church fhall rife to a ftate of beauty and glory, of which Solomon's temple was a type, when the meek fhall inherit the earth, and delight themfelves in the abundance of peace.

The coming of Chrift, in favour of his church and of the redeemed, is fpoken of as a time of vengeance to his and their enemies, in which they fhall be punifhed and deftroyed, and his people fhall be avenged on them. " The Spirit of the Lord God is upon me, becaufe he hath anointed me to preach good tidings unto the meek ; to proclaim the acceptable year of the Lord, *and the day of vengeance of our God,* to comfort all that mourn. " For the day of vengeance is in mine heart, and the year of my redeemed is come."* " And fhall not God avenge his own elect, who cry day and night unto him, though he bear long with them : I tell you that he will avenge them fpeedily."† "Rejoice over her, thou heaven, and ye holy Apoftles, and Prophets ; for God hath avenged you on her. And I heard a great voice of much people in heaven, faying, Hallelujah ! Salvation, and glory, and honour, and power unto the Lord our God : For true and righteous are his judgments ; for he hath judged the great whore, which did corrupt the earth with her fornication, and hath avenged the blood of his fervants at her hand."‡

Balaam, in his remarkable prophecy of Chrift and his kingdom, fpeaking of this latter day, when the Roman empire fhall come to an end, and Chrift fhall have the dominion, reprefents this event as attended with great deftruction of men. " Out of Jacob fhall come he that fhall have dominion, and fhall deftroy him that remaineth in the city. And he took up his parable, and faid, "Alas, who fhall live when God doth this !" This expreffes a great and general deftruction of men, fo that comparatively few of them will be left alive.§  The fame is predicted in the fong which God directed

Q

rected

---

* Ifai. lxi. 1, 2. lxiii. 4.    † Luke xviii. 7, 8.
‡ Rev. xviii. 20, xix. 1, 2.    § Numb. xxiv. 17—24.

rected Mofes to rehearfe to the children of Ifrael, to be preferved by them.* "For I lift my hand to heaven, and fay, I live forever. If (or when) I whet my glittering fword, and mine hand take hold on judgment I will render vengeance to mine enemies, and will reward them that hate me. I will make mine arrows drunk with their blood (and my fword fhall devour flefh) and that with the blood of the flain, and of the captives, from the beginning of revenges upon the enemy. Rejoice, O ye nations, with his people ; for he will avenge the blood of his fervants, and will render vengeance to his adverfaries, and will be merciful unto his land, and to his people." This prophecy is very parallel with that which has been mentioned, which relates to the great battle.† The fame events are predicted in the following words of Mofes : "There is none like unto the God of Jefhurun, who rideth upon the heaven in thy help, and in his excellency on the fky. The eternal God is thy refuge, and underneath are the everlafting arms : And he fhall thruft out the enemy from before thee, and fhall fay, Deftroy them. Ifrael then fhall dwell in fafety alone. The fountain of Jacob fhall be upon a land of corn and wine ; alfo his heavens fhall drop down dew."‡ In thefe words, God is reprefented as riding forth to thruft out and deftroy the enemies of his people ; and upon this the profperity of his church, the true Ifrael, is introduced. This prophecy therefore coincides with the defcription of the battle in the Revelation, as introductory to the Millennium. The fame events are predicted in the prayer or fong of Hannah. "He will keep the feet of his faints, and the wicked fhall be filent in darknefs ; for by ftrength fhall no man prevail. The adverfaries of the Lord fhall be broken to pieces : Out of heaven fhall he thunder upon them. The Lord fhall judge the ends of the earth, and he fhall give ftrength unto his king, and exalt the horn of his anointed."§

This battle, by which the wicked will be deftroyed, and the reign of Chrift and his church on earth introduced, is frequently brought into view and predicted in the book of Pfalms. The following predictions of this kind, are worthy to be obferved :— "Afk of me, and I will give thee the heathen for thine inheritance, and the utmoft parts of the earth for thy poffeffion. Thou fhalt break them with a rod of iron, thou fhalt dafh them in pieces like

---

* Deut. xxxii. 40, 41, 42, 43.      † Rev. xviii. 20. xix 1, 2.
‡ Deut. xxxiii. 26, 27, 28.      § 1 Sam. ii. 9, 10.

like a potter's veſſel."* There is reference to this prediction and promiſe in the following words of Chriſt : " And he that overcometh, and keepeth my works unto the end, to him will I give power over the nations ; and he ſhall rule them with a rod of iron ; as the veſſels of a potter ſhall they be broken to pieces, even as I received of my Father."† The followers of Chriſt are ſaid to do what he does for them, and in their behalf in deſtroying their enemies, as they are engaged in the ſame cauſe, and are with him in theſe works of vengeance, and they who have overcome, and have arrived to heaven, will be with him in a peculiar manner, when he ſhall come forth to fight this great battle, and daſh the nations of the world into pieces, as a potter's veſſel is broken. Therefore, there is again reference to thoſe words in the ſecond Pſalm, when Chriſt is repreſented as riding forth to the battle there deſcribed, followed by the armies in heaven, comprehending all who ſhall then have overcome. " And out of his mouth goeth a ſharp ſword, that with it he ſhould ſmite the nations : And he ſhall rule them with a rod of iron : And he treadeth the wine preſs of the fierceneſs and wrath of Almighty God."‡ This is certainly the ſame with the battle of that great day of Almighty God, mentioned in the ſixteenth chapter, as has been ſhown ; and is predicted in the words now quoted from the ſecond Pſalm.— There is a prediction of the ſame battle deſcribed in the nineteenth chapter of the Revelation, in the following words : " Gird thy ſword upon thy thigh, O moſt mighty ; with thy glory and thy majeſty. And in thy majeſty ride proſperouſly, becauſe of truth and meekneſs, and righteouſneſs : And thy right hand ſhall teach thee terrible things. Thine arrows are ſharp in the heart of the king's enemies, whereby the people fall under thee."§ In the next Pſalm, the proſperity of the church is predicted, which will take place in the Millennium ; and the battle by which it will be introduced and effected is alſo deſcribed. " There is a river, the ſtreams whereof ſhall make glad the city of our God. God is in the midſt of her ; ſhe ſhall not be moved : God ſhall help her, and that right early. The heathen raged, the kingdoms were moved : He uttered his voice, the earth melted. Come, behold the works of the Lord, what deſolations he hath made in the earth. He maketh wars to ceaſe unto the end of the earth, he breaketh the bow, and cutteth the ſpear in ſunder, he burneth the chariot

in

---

* Pſal. ii. 8, 9.        † Rev. ii. 26, 27.
‡ Rev. xix. 14, 15.     § Pſal. xlv. 3, 4, 5.

in the fire. Be ftill, and know that I am God : I will be exalted among the heathen, I will be exalted in the earth."

The twenty firft Pfalm contains a prediction of Chrift, and foretells the deftruction of the wicked, as introducing his reign on earth, and the profperity and joy of the church. "Thine hand fhall find out all thine enemies, thy right hand fhall find out thofe that hate thee. Thou fhalt make them as a fiery oven in the time of thine anger : The Lord fhall fwallow them up in his wrath, and the fire fhall devour them. Their fruit fhalt thou deftroy from the earth, and their feed from among the children of men : For they intended evil againft thee ; they imagined a mifchievous device, which they are not able to perform. Therefore fhalt thou make them turn their back, when thou fhalt make ready thine arrows upon thy ftrings, againft the face of them. Be thou exalted, Lord, in thine own ftrength : So fhall we fing and praife thy power."*

That the wicked fhall be cut off and deftroyed from the earth, that the faints may inherit it, is foretold throughout the thirty feventh Pfalm. "Evil doers fhall be cut off : But thofe that wait upon the Lord, they fhall inherit the earth. For yet a little while, and the wicked fhall not be : Yea, thou fhalt diligently confider his place, and it fhall not be. But the meek fhall inherit the earth, and delight themfelves in the abundance of peace. Wait on the Lord, and keep his way, and he fhall exalt thee to inherit the earth : When the wicked are cut off, thou fhalt fee it. The tranfgreffors fhall be deftroyed together ; the end of the wicked fhall be cut off. But the falvation of the righteous is of the Lord," &c.

The fame thing is brought into view in the feventy fifth, feventy fixth, and ninety feventh Pfalms. "God is the judge, he putteth down one, and fetteth up another. For in the hand of the Lord there is a cup, and the wine is red ; it is full of mixture, and he poureth out of the fame ; but the dregs thereof, all the wicked of the earth fhall wring them out, and drink them. All the horns of the wicked alfo will I cut off ; but the horns of the righteous fhall be exalted. In Judah, is God known, his name is great in Ifrael. In Salem alfo is his tabernacle, and his dwelling place in Zion. There brake he the arrows of the bow, the fhield, and the fword, and the battle. Thou art more glorious and excellent than

the

* Verf. 8—13.

the mountains of prey. The ftout hearted are fpoiled, they have flept their fleep : And none of the men of might have found their hands. At thy rebuke, O God of Jacob, both the chariot and horfe are caft into a dead fleep. Thou didft caufe judgment to be heard from heaven ; the earth feared and was ftill, when God arofe to judgment, to fave all the meek of the earth. He fhall cut off the fpirit of princes : He is terrible to the kings of the earth." " The Lord reigneth, let the people rejoice ; let the multitude of ifles be glad thereof. Clouds and darknefs are round about him, righteoufnefs and judgment are the habitation of his throne. A fire goeth before him, and burneth up his enemies round about. His lightnings enlightned the world : The earth faw, and trembled. The hills melted like wax at the prefence of the Lord ; at the prefence of the Lord of the whole earth. Confounded be all they that ferve graven images, that boaft themfelves of idols.— Worfhip him all ye gods." This battle is brought into view, and foretold in the 110th Pfalm. " The Lord faid unto my Lord, fit thou at my right hand, until I make thine enemies thy footftool. The Lord fhall fend the rod of thy ftrength out of Zion ; rule thou in the midft of thine enemies. The Lord at thy right hand fhall ftrike through kings in the day of his wrath, (i. e. in the great day of battle ) He fhall judge among the heathen, he fhall fill the places with the dead bodies ; he fhall wound the heads over many countries."

In the prophecy of Ifaiah, this battle, as it has been explained, is often brought into view, as connected with the profperity of the church of Chrift on earth, and introductory to it : Some inftances of this will be mentioned. In the five firft verfes of the fecond chapter, there is a prophecy of the happy ftate of the church in the laft days, that is, in the Millennium. In the four next verfes is a defcription of the corruption, worldlinefs and idolatry of the vifible church, and confequently of the world in general, as the reafon of the difpleafure with them, and his punifhing them. And from the tenth verfe to the end of the chapter, the manifeftation of his difpleafure, in his fighting againft them, and punifhing them, is defcribed. " Enter into the rock, and hide thee in the duft, for fear of the Lord, and for the glory of his majefty. The lofty looks of man fhall be humbled, and the haughtinefs of men fhall be bowed down, and the Lord alone fhall be exalted in that day. For the day of the Lord of hofts fhall be upon every one that is

proud

proud and lofty, and upon every one that is lifted up, and he shall be brought low. And the idols he shall utterly abolish. And they shall go into the holes of the rocks, and into the caves of the earth, for fear of the Lord, and for the glory of his majesty, when he ariseth to shake terribly the earth·"

The eleventh chapter contains a prediction of the Millennium, and of the slaughter of the wicked of the earth, which shall make way for it. "With righteousness shall he judge the poor, and reprove with equity, for the meek of the earth: And he shall smite the earth with the rod of his mouth, and with the breath of his lips shall he slay the wicked."* These last words are parellel with those in the Revelation, by which this battle, and the effect of it are expressed. "And out of his mouth goeth a sharp sword, that with it he should smite the nations, and he shall rule them with a rod of iron: And the remnant were slain with the sword of him who sat on the horse, which sword proceedeth out of his mouth."†

In the thirteenth chapter is a prediction of the same thing: "Howl ye, for the day of the Lord is at hand; it shall come as a destruction from the Almighty. Behold, the day of the Lord cometh, cruel both with wrath, and fierce anger, to lay the earth desolate :· And he shall destroy the sinners thereof out of it. And will punish the world for their evil, and the wicked for their iniquity ; and I will cause the arrogancy of the proud to cease, and will lay low the haughtiness of the terrible."‡ What is said in this chapter, has reference to ancient Babylon, and the destruction of that, and of other nations, in order to the deliverance and restoration of Israel. But it evidently has chief reference to the destruction of spiritual Babylon, and all the wicked in the world, in order to the deliverance and prosperity of the true, spiritual Israel of God, and will be most completely fulfilled in the latter, of which the former are types and shadows. As those prophecies which have a primary respect to the type, do generally, if not always, look forward to the antitype; and have their full and chief accomplishment in that, and the events which relate to it.

The twenty fourth chapter is wholly on this subject, and describes the battle of that great day of God Almighty, and the slaughter of the wicked, in clear and striking language, in consequence of which, the church and people of God shall spread and prosper.

* Verse 4.    † Rev. xix. 15, 21.    ‡ Verse 6—11.

profper. " Behold, the Lord maketh the earth empty, and maketh
it wafte, and turneth it upfide down, and fcattereth abroad the inhabitants thereof.   The earth fhall be utterly emptied ; for the
Lord hath fpoken this word.   The earth mourneth and fadeth
away : The world languifheth and fadeth away : The haughty
people of the earth do languifh.   The earth is alfo defiled under
the inhabitants thereof, becaufe they have tranfgreffed the laws,
changed the ordinance, broken the everlafting covenant.   Therefore hath the curfe devoured the earth, and they who dwell therein
are defolate : Therefore the inhabitants of the earth are burned,
and few men left.   The city of confufion is broken down : Every
houfe is fhut up, that no man may remain.   In the city is left defolation, and the gate is fmitten with deftruction.   When thus it
fhall be, in the midft of the earth, among the people, there fhall
be as the fhaking of an olive tree, and as the gleaning of grapes,
when the vintage is done.   They fhall lift up the voice, they fhall
fing for the majefty of the Lord," &c.

Upon this prophecy it may be obferved, that it is a prediction
of great calamities on the inhabitants of the world in general, as a
punifhment for their fins, by which the earth is defiled ; they having tranfgreffed the laws of God, changed his ordinance, and
broken the everlafting covenant.   They have broken the covenant
of grace and peace, made with Noah and his children, which, if
it had been ftrictly obferved, would have tranfmitted bleffings,
both holinefs and happinefs, to all mankind, to the end of the
world.   By violating this covenant, corruption and iniquity, and
all the idolatry and abominations which have taken place, or ever
will be practifed among men, have been introduced.   And by
breaking the everlafting covenant made with Abraham, and tranf-
greffing the laws, and changing the ordinances, which have been
given and publifhed by Mofes, and the Prophets, by Jefus Chrift,
and his Apoftles, which, had they been obferved, would have preferved the church uncorrupt, and fpread true religion and holinefs
over the whole earth ; by difregarding and violating all thefe, the
world is filled with wickednefs, which will continue and increafe,
until mankind in general fhall be ripe for that punifhment, which
God will inflict in thofe calamities and judgments, which will deftroy, and fweep from the earth, the greateft part of the inhabitants ; fo that there will be but comparatively *few men left*, like the
few olives which remain on the tree, after it is fhaken, and the fcattering

tering grapes, which hang on the vine, after the vintage is over. Thofe who fhall be left when the battle is over, will lift up their voice, and fing for the majefty of the Lord. They will behold the terrible works of God, in which they will fee his terrible majefty, and tremble, fubmit, approve, and adore, and praife and pray. And then the Millennium will begin.

The prophecy goes on, and the fame events, as to fubftance, and this battle, and the confequence of it, are defcribed in other words : " Fear and the pit, and the fnare are upon thee, O inhabitant of the earth. The earth is utterly broken down, the earth is clean diffolved, the earth is moved exceedingly. The earth fhall reel to and fro like a drunkard, and fhall be moved like a cottage, and the tranfgreffion thereof fhall be heavy upon it, and it fhall fall, and not rife again." This battle is defcribed in the Revelation, in the fame figurative language : " And there was a great earthquake, fuch as was not fince men were upon the earth, fo mighty an earthquake and fo great. And every ifland fled away, and the mountains were not found."* " And it fhall come come to pafs in that day, that the Lord fhall punifh the hoft of the high ones that are on high, and the kings of the earth upon the earth. And they fhall be gathered together as prifoners are gathered in the pit, and fhall be fhut up in the prifon ; and after many days fhall they be vifited.† Then the moon fhall be confounded, and the fun afhamed, when the Lord of hofts fhall reign in Mount Zion, and in Jerufalem, and before his ancients glorioufly." This prediction refpects the great men and kings of the earth, who exalt

* Rev. xvi. 18, 20.

† What is meant by the hoft of the high ones, and the kings of the earth being *vifited* after many days, is not fo clear, at firft view, and perhaps it is not now underftood. God is often faid in fcripture to *vifit* thofe whom he punifhes, and the word here in the original is frequently tranflated, to punifh. They who are fhut up in prifon, are often confined there, to be taken out after fome days, and receive their punifhment. When it is here faid, " And after many days fhall they be vifited ;" may not the meaning be, that thofe high ones, and kings of the earth fhall no more appear in this world ; but fhall be fhut up in prifon until the day of judgment, when they fhall be brought forth and punifhed ? As the fallen angels are bound in chains of darknefs to be referved unto judgment, fo thefe unjuft men will be referved unto the day of judgment, to be punifhed. When it is faid of Zedekiah, that he fhould be carried a captive to Babylon, it is added, " And there fhall he be, until I vifit him, faith the Lord." Jer. xxxii. 5. That is, until God fhould take him out of the world by death, and to judgment ; fo that he fhould never reign as king any more.

alt themfelves in pride and wickednefs, and tyrannize over men,
and defcribes their overthrow in this battle. They fhall be taken
as prifoners, be punifhed for their pride and tyranny, and fhut up
that they may do no more mifchief. Thus God " will cut off the
fpirit of princes, and be terrible to the kings of the earth."\* And
it is here faid, that the Millennium fhall follow upon this, in the
reign of Chrift and his church, " When the Lord of hofts fhall
reign in Mount Zion, and in Jerufalem, and before his ancients
glorioufly." " Then the moon fhall be confounded, and the fun
afhamed." That is, then there fhall be fuch fpiritual light and
glory in the flourifhing of the kingdom of Chrift on earth, and
fo fuperiour to all the light and glory of the natural world, as that
the latter fhall be utterly eclipfed, and appear to be worthy of no
regard, compared with the former.

The three next chapters are a continuation of prophecy of the
fame event, viz. the judgments which are to be inflicted on the
falfe and degenerate profeffors of religion, and the world of mankind in general, previous to the profperity of the church and kingdom of Chrift in the world, which will be evident to the careful
judicious reader ; and that the predictions contained in them,
coincide with thofe which have been mentioned. It is needlefs
to tranfcribe any particular paffage here, except the following :—
" Come, my people, enter thou into thy chambers, and fhut thy
doors about thee ; hide thyfelf as it were for a little moment, until the indignation be overpaffed. For behold, the Lord cometh
out of his place to punifh the inhabitants of the earth for their
iniquity : The earth alfo fhall difclofe her blood, and fhall no more
cover her flain."† This muft be a great and dreadful day of battle, punifhment and vengeance, which fhall fall on the inhabitants
of the earth in general, when all the blood which has been, and
fhall be fhed, from the beginning of the world to that day, fhall
be required at their hands. There is no reafon to think, that
this punifhment has yet been inflicted ; but it will doubtlefs be
executed by the battle of that great day of God Almighty, mentioned in the fixteenth chapter of the Revelation ; and more particularly defcribed, in the fourteenth and nineteenth chapters, which
have been confidered ; and in the foregoing prophecies of Ifaiah,
which have been now mentioned. The words which follow
thofe tranfcribed above, are, " In that day, the Lord with his

R                                      fore

\* Pfal. lxxvi. 12.        † Ifai. xxvi. 20, 21.

fore great and ftrong fword, fhall punifh leviathan the piercing ferpent, even leviathan that crooked ferpent, and he fhall flay the dragon that is in the fea." The fame event is here predicted, of which there is a prophecy in the twentieth chapter of the Revelation, viz. of the dragon that old ferpent, which is the devil and fatan, being laid hold of, and bound and caft into the bottomlefs pit. And the fame confequence of this with refpect to the church is here foretold, as is defcribed there, viz. the profperity of it, by the fpecial favour and prefence of God. "In that day fing ye unto her, A vineyard of red wine. I the Lord do keep it, I will water it every moment : Left any hurt it, I will keep it night and day." While the battle is going on, and God is punifhing the inhabitants of the earth for their iniquity, his people will be hid as in a fecret chamber ; but when it is over, they will become as a flourifhing, fruitful vineyard, producing abundance of red wine, in confequence of the peculiar favour and care of Jefus Chrift, and the abundance of heavenly divine influences.

The thirty fourth, and thirty fifth chapters of Ifaiah, contain a prophecy of the Millennium, and of the day of battle which will precede it, which will confift in the punifhment of the world for their iniquity. " Come near, ye nations, to hear, and hearken, ye people :` Let the earth hear, and all that is therein ; the world, and all things that come forth of it. For the indignation of the Lord is upon all nations, and his fury upon all their armies. He hath utterly deftroyed them, he hath delivered them to the flaughter. For it is the day of the Lord's vengeance, and the year of recompences for the controverfy of Zion. Strengthen ye the weak hands, confirm the feeble knees. Say to them that are of a fearful heart, Be ftrong, fear not : Behold, your God will come with vengeance, even God with a recompence ; he will come and fave you. Then the eyes of the blind fhall be opened, and the ears of the deaf fhall be unftopped. Then fhall the lame man leap as an hart, and the tongue of the dumb fhall fing ; for in the wildernefs fhall waters break out, and ftreams in the defert," &c " And the ranfomed of the Lord fhall return and come to Zion with fongs, and everlafting joy upon their heads ; they fhall obtain joy and gladnefs, and forrow and fighing fhall flee away."

In the forty firft chapter of Ifaiah, God, fpeaking to the church, and promifing the good things and profperity which were in ftore

for

for it in the days of the Millennium, fays, " Behold, all they that
are incenfed againft thee, fhall be afhamed and confounded :
They fhall be as nothing, and they that ftrive with thee, fhall
perifh.   Thou fhalt feek them, and fhall not find them that contended with thee :  They that war againft thee, fhall be as nothing,
and as a thing of nought.    Behold, I will make thee a new,
fharp threfhing inftrument, having teeth ; thou fhall threfh the
mountains, and beat them fmall, and make the hills as chaff.
Thou fhalt fan them, and the wind fhall carry them away, and
the whirlwind fhall fcatter them :  And thou fhalt rejoice in the
Lord, and fhalt glory in the Holy One of Ifrael."

    In the forty fecond chapter, God makes promifes to his church,
which are to be accomplifhed in their fulnefs, in the days of the
Millennium, and fpeaks of the war and battle in which he will
deftroy his enemies, to open the way for the good thing which
was to be done for the church.   " The Lord fhall go forth as a
mighty man, he fhall ftir up jealoufy like a man of war :  He fhall
cry, yea, roar ; he fhall prevail againft his enemies.   I have long
time holden my peace, I have been ftill, and refrained myfelf : Now
will I cry like a travailing woman, I will deftroy and devour at
once.   I will make wafte mountains and hills, and dry up all their
herbs ; and I will make the rivers iflands, and I will dry up the
pools.   And I will bring the blind by a way that they knew not,
I will lead them in paths that they have not known :  I will make
darknefs light before them, and crooked things ftraight.   Thefe
things will I do unto them, and not forfake them."

    The fifty ninth and fixtieth chapters, are wholly on this fubject
of the Millennium.   In the fourteen firft verfes of the fifty ninth
chapter, the great degree of wickednefs of the world of mankind
is defcribed.   And then God is reprefented as greatly difpleafed,
and rifing to battle, to punifh men for their evil deeds.   " And
the Lord faw it, and it difpleafed him that there was no judgment.
And he faw that there was no man, and he wondered that there
was no interceffor :  Therefore, his arm brought falvation unto
him, and his righteoufnefs, it fuftained him.   For he put on righteoufnefs as a breaftplate, and an helmit of falvation upon his
head ; and he put on the garments of vengeance for clothing,
and was clad with zeal as a cloke.   According to their deeds,
accordingly he will repay, fury to. his adverfaries, recompence to
his enemies ; to the iflands he will repay recompence.   So fhall

               R 2                              they

they fear the name of the Lord from the weſt, and his glory from the riſing of the ſun. When the enemy ſhall come in like a flood, the Spirit of the Lord ſhall lift up a ſtandard againſt him." And to this battle, this work of judgment and vengeance, ſucceeds the day of light and ſalvation to the church : Thoſe who are left, ſhall repent and humble themſelves, and "fear the name of the Lord from the weſt, and his glory from the riſing of the ſun. And the Redeemer ſhall come to Zion, and to them that turn from tranſgreſſion in Jacob." It will be then ſaid to the church, " Ariſe, ſhine, for thy light is come, and the glory of the Lord is riſen upon thee."—The prophecy of the Millennium goes on through the ſixtieth, ſixty firſt, and ſixty ſecond chapters.

There is a parallel repreſentation of this battle in the ſixty third chapter, as executed by the ſame perſon who is exhibited in the nineteenth chapter of the Revelation, riding forth to make war in righteouſneſs, and fighting this ſame battle, in which the wicked then on earth will be ſlain. "Who is this that cometh from Edom, with died garments from Bozrah ?* This who is glorious in his apparel, travelling in the greatneſs of his ſtrength ? I who ſpeak in righteouſneſs, mighty to ſave. Wherefore art thou red in thine apparel, and thy garments like him who treadeth in the wine fat ? I have trodden the wine preſs alone, and of the people there was none with me : For I will tread them in mine anger, and trample them in my fury, and the blood ſhall be ſprinked upon my garments, and I will ſtain all my raiment. For the day of vengeance is in my heart, and the year of my redeemed is come. And I looked, and there was none to help, and I wondered that there was none to uphold : Therefore, mine own arm brought ſalvation unto me, and my fury it upheld me. And I will tread down the people in mine anger, and make them drunk in my fury, and I will bring down their ſtrength to the earth."

The ſame thing is predicted in the ſixty ſixth chapter: " A voice of noiſe from the city, a voice from the temple, a voice of the Lord who rendereth recompence to his enemies. And the hand of the Lord ſhall be known towards his ſervants, and his indignation

---

* Bozrah was in the land of Edom. The Edomites, were implacable enemies to the people of God, and are in the prophecies of Iſaiah, and elſewhere, put for the enemies of God and his church in general, who ſhall be deſtroyed, as the Edomites were, of whom the Edomites, and their deſtruction were a type.

dignation towards his enemies.  For behold, the Lord will come with fire, and with his chariots like a whirlwind, to render his anger with fury, and his rebuke with flames of fire.  For by fire, and by his fword, will the Lord plead with all flefh; and the flain of the Lord fhall be many."  Thefe predictions of the flaughter and deftruction of the wicked, are here intermixed with promifes of falvation and profperity to the church : " Rejoice ye with Jerufalem, and be glad with her, all ye who love her : Rejoice for joy with her, all ye that mourn for her : That ye may fuck and be fatisfied with the breafts of her confolations : That ye may milk out, and be delighted with the abundance of her glory.  For thus faith the Lord, Behold, I will extend peace to her like a river, and the glory of the Gentiles like a flowing ftream.  And when ye fee this, your heart fhail rejoice, and your bones fhall flourifh like an herb."

A paffage in the tenth chapter of Jeremiah, feems to refer to the fame event.  The folly, idolatry, and great wickednefs of the people and nations of the earth, is mentioned and defcribed in the firft part of the chapter, upon which the following prediction is uttered : But Jehovah is the true God, he is the living God, and an everlafting King : At his wrath the earth fhall tremble, and the nations fhall not be able to abide his indignation.  Thus fhall ye fay unto them, The gods that have not made the heavens, and the earth, even they fhall perifh from the earth, and from under thofe heavens."

In the firft part of the twenty fifth chapter, there is a prophecy of the captivity of the Jews, and of other adjacent nations, by Nebuchadnezzar ; and when their captivity during feventy years fhould be ended, Jeremiah foretells the ruin of Babylon, and the land of the Chaldeans.  And the evil that was coming on the nations of the earth, which fhould attend the deftruction of Babylon, is reprefented by ordering Jeremiah to take the wine cup of wrath, and caufe all the nations of the earth to drink of it.  And as the deftruction of ancient Babylon, and the judgments which came on many other nations, was an eminent type of yet greater and more remarkable deftruction of fpiritual Babylon, and of all the nations of the earth, which will attend that, the prophecy is carried on beyond the type, and looks forward to the antitype, which is common in fcripture prophecy ; and expreffions are ufed which cannot be applied to the former, to the type, in their full extent

and

and meaning, but to the latter, the antitype, and therefore the prophecy is accomplished but in part, and in a lower degree in the former; but fully and moſt completely in the latter: Therefore, the Prophet goes on, and uſes expreſſions toward the cloſe of the prophecy, which refer chiefly to the battle in which antichriſt, and the nations of the earth will fall. Such are the following: " Therefore, propheſy thou againſt them all thoſe words, and ſay unto them, The Lord ſhall roar from on high, and utter his voice from his holy habitation; he ſhall mightiiy roar upon his habitation, he ſhall give a ſhout, as they that tread the grapes, a-gainſt all the inhabitants of the earth. A noiſe ſhall come even to the ends of the earth: For the Lord hath a controverſy with the nations: He will plead with all fleſh, he will give them that are wicked to the ſword, ſaith the Lord. Thus ſaith the Lord of hoſts, Behold, evil ſhall go forth from nation to nation, and a great whirlwind ſhall be raiſed up from the coaſts of the earth. And the ſlain of the Lord ſhall be at that day, from one end of 'the earth, even unto the other end of the earth: They ſhall not be lamented, neither gathered, nor buried; they ſhall be dung upon the ground."* The Prophet goes on to predict the evil that ſhould come on the ſhepherds, and the principal of the flock, by whom are meant the kings and great men among the nations, who are to be brought down and deſtroyed in the battle,† which is agreeable to the forementioned prophecy in Iſaiah,‡ and to the repreſentation of the ſame battle in the Revelation.§

There is another prophecy of this in the thirtieth chapter of Jeremiah. Here the deliverance of the church from her oppreſſors, and from all her ſufferings and trouble, is promiſed; which ſhall be attended with the utter overthrow and deſtruction of the wick-ed, and all her enemies. That this prophecy looks beyond the deliverance of the Jews from the Babyloniſh captivity, and the evil that came on their enemies then, to the greater deliverance of the church from ſpiritual Babylon, and the general deſtruction of the wicked which ſhall attend it, of which the former was a type, is evident, not only from a number of expreſſions and promiſes which were not fully accompliſhed in the former, and have re-ſpect to the latter; but from the expreſs promiſe, that God will raiſe up David their king to reign over them, by whom muſt be

meant

* Verſe 30—33.  † Verſe 34—38.
‡ Chap. xxiv. 2ɪ, 22.  § Rev. xix. 18.

meant Jefus Chrift, the Son of David, and of whom David was an eminent type. This will appear, by attending to the following paffages : " Alas! For that day is great, fo that none is like it : It is even the time of Jacob's trouble ; but he fhall be delivered out of it. For it fhall come to pafs in that day, faith the Lord of hofts, that I will break his yoke from off thy neck, and will burft thy bonds, and ftrangers fhall no more ferve themfelves of him. But they fhall ferve the Lord their God, and David their king, whom I will raife up unto them. For I am with thee, faith the Lord, to fave thee. Though I make a full end of all nations whither I have fcattered thee, yet I will not make a full end of thee. Behold, a whirlwind of the Lord goeth forth with fury, a continuing whirlwind, it fhall fall with pain upon the head of the wicked. The fierce anger of the Lord fhall not return, until he have done it, and until he have performed the intents of his heart : In the latter days ye fhall confider it."*

In the book of Daniel, there is prophecy of the fame event. "And at that time," (i. e. when antichrift is to be deftroyed, which is predicted in the paragraph immediately preceding thefe words) " fhall Michael ftand up, the great Prince who ftandeth for the children of thy people" (that is, Jefus Chrift, who will fupport and deliver his church) " And there fhall be a time of trouble, fuch as never was fince there was a nation, even to that fame time," (this is the time of the battle of that great day of God Almighty) " And at that time, thy people fhall be delivered, every one that fhall be found written in the book." This is the time of the deliverance of the church from the power of antichrift, and from all wicked men, her enemies, and of her entering upon the profperous, happy ftate, in which the faints will reign on earth a thoufand years.

The Prophet Joel fpeaks of the fame events. From the twenty eighth verfe of the fecond chapter of his prophecy, is a prediction of the Millennium, and the preceding evils that fhall be inflicted on mankind : " And it fhall come to pafs afterwards, that I will pour out my Spirit upon all flefh," &c. " This prophecy began to be fulfilled, when the Holy Spirit was firft poured out after the afcention of Chrift ; but this, as has been before obferved, was but the firft fruits, and the prophecy will be fulfilled only in a very fmall part, before the harveft fhall come in the days of the Millennium.

At

* Verfes 7, 8, 9, 11, 23, 24.

At the fame time he fpeaks of the great evils, and terrible events which fhall take place : " The fun fhall be turned into darknefs, and the moon into blood, before the great and terrible day of the Lord come. And it fhall come to pafs, that whofoever fhall call on the name of the Lord, fhall be delivered." The Prophet goes on in the next chapter to fpeak more particularly on this fubject : " For behold, in thofe days and in that time, when I fhall bring a-gain the captivity of Judah, and Jerufalem, I will alfo gather all nations, and will bring them down into the valley of Jehofhaphat, and will plead with them there for my people, and for my heritage Ifrael, whom they have fcattered among the nations, and parted my land."

Judah and Jerufalem are put for the church of Chrift, being a type of that, as has been obferved. The captivity of the Jews in Babylon, and their return from it, is typical of the afflicted, fuffer-ing ftate of the church during the reign of antichrift, and the de-liverance of it from this ftate on the fall of antichrift, and in the Millennium. This is therefore meant, when it is faid, " In thofe days, and in that time, when I fhall bring again the captivity of Judah and Jerufalem." When the children of Moab, Ammon, and Edom, came with a great army, combined together to deftroy Judah, Jehofhaphat was directed to go forth with the inhabitants of Judah and Jerufalem and meet them ; and had a promife that he fhould have no occafion to fight with them ; but fhould ftand ftill and fee the falvation of the Lord, becaufe the battle was not their's, but God's. Accordingly they went out, and ftood ftill, and faw their enemies fall upon, and deftroy each other, until they were all wafted away. Jehofhaphat and his people went out to their camp, and found great riches, filver and gold, and much fpoil ; and they fpent three days in gathering it ; and on the fourth day they affembled in the valley to blefs and praife the Lord, which was from that called, " The valley of Berachah." This is the valley of Jehofhaphat. And to this ftory, thefe words of the Prophet Joel refer.* Moab, Ammon, and Edom, the enemies of Ifrael, were a type of the enemies of the church and people of God, under the gofpel difpenfation, among all nations. This battle and their deftruction of the enemies of Judah and Jerufalem in the valley of Jehofhaphat, was a type of the overthrow of all the enemies of Chrift and his church, when they fhall be gathered to the battle of

that

* See 2 Chron. 20th Chapter.

that great day of God Almighty. This prophecy therefore, is a prediction of the fame event which is defcribed in the fixteenth chapter of the Revelation. Here it is faid, " I will gather all nations, and will bring them down into the valley of Jehofhaphat, and will plead with them there for my people." That is, will punifh and deftroy them for their oppofition to me and my church. There it is faid, " The kings of the earth and of the whole world, were gathered to the battle of that great day. And he gathered them together to a place called in the Hebrew tongue, Armageddon." Which paffage has been before explained.

The Prophet farther enlarges on this fubject in the following part of this chapter :* Proclaim ye this among the Gentiles : Prepare war, wake up the mighty men, let all the men of war draw near, let them come up. Beat your plowfhares into fwords, and your pruning hooks into fpears ; let the weak fay, I am ftrong. Affemble yourfelves, and come, all ye heathen, and gather yourfelves together round about : Thither caufe thy mighty ones to come down, O Lord. Let the heathen be wakened and come up to the valley of Jehofhaphat ; for there will I fit to judge all the heathen round about. Put ye in the fickle, for the harveft is ripe ; come, get you down, for the prefs is full, the fats overflow, for their wickednefs is great. Multitudes, multitudes, in the valley of decifion ; for the day of the Lord is near in the valley of decifion. The fun and moon fhall be darkened, and the ftars fhall withdraw their fhining. The Lord fhall alfo roar out of Zion, and utter his voice from Jerufalem, and the heavens and the earth fhall fhake ; but the Lord will be the hope of his people, and the ftrength of the children of Ifrael." Every one who attends to this paffage, will obferve what a ftriking fimilitude there is between this defcription of a battle, and that in the Revelation, which has been confidered. God is here reprefented as fighting the battle againft all the heathen, and deftroying multitudes on multitudes. All the heathen, even all nations are gathered together, all armed for war, and come up to the valley of Jehofhaphat, and there are cut off in this valley of decifion. In the Revelation all the nations of the earth are gathered together to battle at Megiddo, typifying the fame thing with the valley of Jehofhaphat, and there they are flain. God caufes his mighty ones to come down. And John fays, " I faw heaven opened, and behold, a white horfe

S                                                        And

* Verfe 9, &c.

And he that fat upon him was called faithful and true, and in righteoufnefs doth he judge, and make war. And his name is called, The word of God. And the armies in heaven followed him upon white horfes." Here there is a command to " put in the fickle, for the harveft is ripe : Come, get you down, for the prefs is full, the fats overflow, for the wickednefs is great." Much the fame reprefentation is made of this battle in the Revelation,* which has been particularly mentioned already. The Prophet Joel goes on to the end of his prophecy defcribing the happy ftate of the church, which fhall fucceed this battle, which has never yet taken place, and is like other defcriptions of the Millennium ftate, by the Prophets. " Then fhall Jerufalem be holy, and there fhall no ftranger pafs through her any more. And it fhall come to pafs in that day, that the mountains fhall drop down new wine, and the hills fhall flow with milk. Egypt fhall be a defolation, and Edom fhall be a defolate wildernefs, for the violence againft the children of Judah, becaufe they have fhed innocent blood in their land. But Judah fhall dwell forever, and Jerufalem from generation to generation."

The Prophet Micah, prophefied of Chrift and his kingdom, in the extent and glory of it in the latter day ; and of the deftruction of the wicked men, and the nations of the world, in favour of the church of Chrift, and in order to the profperity of his people.— All this is contained in the fifth chapter of his prophecy. " And He (i. e. Chrift) fhall ftand and feed in the ftrength of the Lord, in the majefty of the name of the Lord his God : And they fhall abide ; for now fhall he be great unto the ends of the earth. And the remnant of Jacob fhall be among the Gentiles, in the midft of many people, as a lion among the beafts of the foreft, as a young lion among the flocks of fheep ; who if he go through, both treadeth down, and teareth in pieces, and none can deliver. Thine hand fhall be lift up upon thine adverfaries, and all thine enemies fhall be cut off. And I will execute vengeance in anger and fury upon the heathen, fuch as they have not heard."†

The prophecy of Zephaniah has refpect to the battle of that great day of God Almighty, and the fucceeding happy and profperous ftate of the church in the Millennium. It has indeed a primary refpect to the evils and punifhment brought upon Jerufalem and the Jews by the Chaldeans, for their apoftacy and idolatry ;

* Chap. xiv. 14, &c.     † Verfes 4, 8, 9, 15,

atry ; and to the calamities and deſtruction which came upon the nations at that time, and previous to the reſtoration of the Jews ; and to their reſtoration from their captivity, and return to their own land ; which were types of the much greater and more important events, in the laſt days, in which all nations will be more immediately concerned ; and to which the prophecy has an ultimate and chief reſpect.  It was fulfilled but in part, and in a ſmall degree, in the former events ; and will have the chief and complete accompliſhment in the latter ; as has been before obſerved concerning other prophecies of the ſame kind.  Jeruſalem in her moſt pure ſtate, when the ſtatutes and ordinances which God had preſcribed, were in ſome good degree obſerved, was a type of the true church of Chriſt.  Therefore, under this name, and that of Mount Zion, and Iſrael, the Prophets ſpeak of the true church in all future ages.  But Jeruſalem, conſidered in her moſt corrupt ſtate of apoſtacy, was a type of the falſe church of Rome, and of all chriſtian churches when they apoſtatize from the holy doctrines and precepts of the goſpel.  Therefore, Chriſt is ſaid to be crucified in the great city, by which is meant the apoſtate church of Rome, and all who partake of her corruptions ; becauſe he was crucified at Jeruſalem, which was then a type of that great city, in her apoſtacy, and enmity againſt Chriſt, and his true church.*  The nations round about the land of Iſrael and Judea, and all thoſe who at times afflicted and oppreſſed the viſible people of God, and were enemies to them ; were types of the enemies of the church of Chriſt, in the time of her affliction ; eſpecially of all the idolatrous nations and wicked men, who oppoſe the proſperity of the church, and are to be deſtroyed, in order to her deliverance and ſalvation.  With theſe obſervations in view, this prophecy may be read, and the whole of it applied to the battle and events which will take place previous to the introduction of the Millennium, predicted in the Revelation, under the ſeventh vial ; and to the proſperity of the church which will then commence.  Then it will have its full accompliſhment ; and many of the expreſſions in it, conſidered in their moſt natural and extenſive meaning, cannot be accommodated to any events which have taken place, and are not yet fulfilled.  Some of theſe will be now mentioned.  The prophecy begins with the following words :—

" I will

* Rev. xi. 8.

"I will utterly comfume all things from off the land,\* faith the
Lord.   I will confume man and beaft : I will confume the fowls
of the heaven, and the fifhes of the fea,  and the ftumbling blocks
with the wicked, and I will cut off man from off the land  (the
earth) faith the Lord.   Hold thy peace at the prefence of the
Lord God :  For the day of the Lord is at hand :  For the Lord
hath prepared a facrifice,  he hath bid his guefts.   The great day
of the Lord is near ;  it is near, and hafteth greatly,  even the voice
of the day of the Lord.   The mighty men fhall cry there bitterly.
That day is a day of wrath, a day of trouble and diftrefs,  a day
of waftenefs and defolation,  a day of darknefs and gloominefs,  a
day of clouds and thick darknefs, a day of the trumpet and alarm
againft the fenced cities, and againft the high towers.   And I will
bring diftrefs upon men, that they fhall walk like blind men,  becaufe they have finned againft the Lord :   And their blood fhall
be poured out as duft, and their flefh as dung.   Neither their filver, nor their gold, fhall be able to deliver them in the day of the
Lord's wrath ;  but the whole land (earth) fhall be devoured by
the fire of his jealoufy :  For he fhall make even a fpeedy riddance
of all them that dwell in the land (earth.)   Seek ye the Lord, all
ye meek of the earth,  which have wrought his judgment ;  feek
righteoufnefs ;  feek meeknefs :  It may be ye fhall be hid in the
day of the Lord's anger.   Therefore, wait upon me, faith the
Lord, until the day that I rife up to the prey ;  for my determination is to gather the nations, that I may affemble the kingdoms,
to pour upon them mine indignation, and all my fierce anger :—
For all the earth fhall be devoured with the fire of my jealoufy."
The parallel and likenefs between this prophecy, and that of the
battle in the Revelation, is worthy of particular notice.   This is
called " The great day of the Lord :  The day of the Lord's
wrath :  A day of diftrefs and defolation :  The day that God will
rife up to the prey, to *gather* the nations, and affemble the kingdoms, to pour upon them his indignation, and fierce anger."—
In the Revelation, the whole world were gathered to the battle of
that great day of God Almighty.   The words, THAT great
day of battle, feem to have reference to fome day which had already

* The word in the original tranflated *land*, is the fame which in other
places in this prophecy, and in many other places in fcripture, is tranflated
*earth*, and doubtlefs fhould have been fo tranflated here, and in fome other
paffages which will be tranfcribed.

ready been made known, and undoubtedly refer to the great day of God's wrath, which is mentioned in the prophecy before us, and by the other Prophets. " And he gathered them together into a place, called in the Hebrew tongue, Armageddon. And the feventh angel poured out his vial (of wrath) into the air. And there were voices, and thunders, and lightnings ; and there was a great earthquake, fuch as was not fince men were upon the earth, fo mighty an earthquake and fo great. And the cities of the nations fell. And great Babylon came in remembrance before God, to give unto her the cup of the wine of the fiercenefs of his wrath. And the remnant were flain with the fword of him who fat on the horfe ; and the fowls were filled with their flefh." In this prophecy it is faid, " The Lord hath prepared a facrifice, he hath bid his guefts." In the Revelation the fowls of heaven are invited to come to the fupper of the great God, to eat the flefh of kings, &c.

According to this Prophet, when the nations and kingdoms of the world have been gathered, and God has poured upon them his indignation, even all his fierce anger ; and all the earth fhall be devoured with the fire of his jealoufy, the fcene is changed, and the remnant which are left in the earth, the few afflicted and poor people, fhall repent and pray, and humble themfelves before God, and return and put their truft in him alone : And God will return to them in a way of mercy, and build them up, and they fhall be comforted, rejoice and profper. This is reprefented in the laft chapter, from verfe ninth to the end of the prophecy : " For then will I turn to the people a pure language, that they may all call upon the name of the Lord, to ferve him with one confent. From beyond the rivers of Ethiopia, my fuppliants, even the daughters of my difperfed, fhall bring mine offering. I will alfo leave in thee an afflicted and poor people, and they fhall truft in the name of the Lord. The remnant of Ifrael fhall not do iniquity, nor fpeak lies ; neither fhall a deceitful tongue be found in their mouth : For they fhall feed and lie down, and none fhall make them afraid. Sing, O daughter of Zion, fhout, O Ifrael, be glad and rejoice with all the heart, O daughter of Jerufalem. The Lord hath taken away thy judgments, he hath caft out thine enemy : The King of Ifrael, even the Lord, is in the midft of thee. Thou fhalt not fee evil any more," &c. to the end of the prophecy.

This

This is set in much the same light in the Revelation.* When the battle there described is over, the Millennium is introduced.

There is a prophecy by the Prophet Haggai to the same purpose with the foregoing : " Again the word of the Lord came unto Haggai, saying, Speak to Zerubbabel, governour of Judah, saying, I will shake the heavens and the earth ; and I will overthrow the throne of kingdoms, and I will destroy the strength of the kingdoms of the heathen, and I will overthrow the chariots, and those who ride in them ; and the horses and their riders shall come down, every one by the sword of his brother. In that day, saith the Lord of hosts, I will take thee, O Zerubbabel my servant, and will make thee as a signet ; for I have chosen thee."† Zerubbabel was a type of Christ, and what is here said of the type was not fulfilled in him ; but is to be fulfilled in Jesus Christ the antitype, when he shall reign on the earth, and his church fill the world, and " he shall be exalted and extolled, and be very high."‡ In order to this, the great changes are to take place, represented here by shaking the heavens and the earth, and by overthrowing the throne and strength of all the kingdoms and nations, and their being destroyed by the sword : Which is the battle represented in the Revelation, by thunders and lightnings, and a great earthquake, and the falling of the cities of the nations, &c.

The Prophet Zechariah also speaks of these things. He prophesies of the Millennium, and of the destruction of all the people and nations who oppose the interest of the church, as preceding the days of her prosperity, and introductory to it. " And in that day will I make Jerusalem (the true church of Christ) a burdensome stone for all people : All that burden themselves with it, shall be cut in pieces, though all the people of the earth be *gathered together* against it. In that day, saith the Lord, I will smite every horse with astonishment, and his rider with madness ; and I will open mine eyes upon the house of Judah, and will smite every horse of the people with blindness. In that day shall the Lord defend the inhabitants of Jerusalem, and he that is feeble among them at that day, shall be as David ; and the house of David shall be as God, as the angel of the Lord before them. And it shall come to pass in that day, that I will seek to destroy all the nations that come against Jerusalem."§ " Behold, the day of the Lord cometh,

---

* Chapters xix, and xx.    † Hagg. ii. 20, 21, 22, 23.
‡ Isai. lii. 13.    § Zech. xii. 3, 4, 8, 9.

cometh, and thy fpoil fhall be divided in the midft of thee.    For
I will gather all nations againft Jerufalem to battle ; and the city
fhall be taken, and the houfes rifled, and the women ravifhed, and
half of the city fhall go forth into captivity, and the refidue of the
people fhall not be cut off from the city." This is the gathering
of the kingdoms and nations of the whole world, unto the battle,
by the unclean fpirits which go forth to corrupt the world, and
arm them againft God, and his people, by the practice of all kinds
of wickednefs, by which the beft part of the church will be greatly
corrupted ; and the faints will fuffer very much, being befieged
on all fides by very wicked men, mentioned in the Revelation,*
which has been explained.

The Prophet goes on to defcribe the battle of that great day of
God Almighty, which is mentioned in the Revelation : " Then
fhall the Lord go forth, and fight againft thofe nations, as when he
fought in the day of battle.    And this fhall be the plague wherewith the Lord will fmite all the people that have fought againft
Jerufalem :  Their .flefh fhall confume away, while they ftand upon their feet, and their eyes fhall confume away in their holes,
and their tongue fhall confume away in their mouth."†

Malachi prophefied of the Millennium, and the preceding
flaughter of the wicked, in the battle of that great day of God Almighty, in the following concife and ftriking language : " Behold
the day cometh that fhall burn as an oven, and all the proud, yea,
and all that do wickedly, fhall be ftubble, and the day that cometh
fhall burn them up, faith the Lord of hofts, that it fhall leave them
neither root nor branch.    But unto you that fear my name, fhall
the fun of righteoufnefs arife with healing in his wings ; and ye
fhall go forth and grow up as calves in the ftall.    And ye fhall
tread down the wicked ; for they fhall be afhes under the foles of
your feet, in the day that I fhall do this, faith the Lord of hofts."‡

FROM the above detail it appears, that the prophecy in the Revelation of the Millennium, and of the manner in which it will be
introduced, is agreeable to the ancient prophecies of thefe fame e-
vents : That previous to this, the chriftian world, and mankind
in general, will become more corrupt in the practice of all kinds of
wickednefs : That God will rife out of his place, and come forth
to do his work, his ftrange work, to punifh the world for their
                                                    wickednefs,

---

* Rev. xvi. 13, 14.    † Verfes 3, 12.    ‡ Mal. iv. 1, 2, 3.

wickednefs, and manifeft his high difpleafure and anger with mankind, for their perverfenefs and obftinacy in rebellion againft him,
and in oppofition to his church : That this is the battle of that
great day of God Almighty, in which he will, by a courfe of various and multiplied calamities and fore judgments, greater and
more general, and continued longer than any which have taken
place before, reduce and deftroy mankind, fo that comparatively
few will be left ; an afflicted and poor people, who will repent and
humble themfelves before God, and truft in the mighty Saviour ;
for whom he will appear in great mercy, and pour down the Holy
Spirit on them and their offspring; and they will multiply and
fill the world. And thus the kingdom and dominion, and the
greatnefs of the kingdom under the whole heaven, fhall be given
to the people of the faints of the Moft High, and the church will
reign on earth a thoufand years.

It appears reafonable and proper, that God fhould manifeft his
difpleafure with the inhabitants of Chriftendom, and of the world,
for their long continued abufe of his goodnefs, and of all the means
ufed with them to reclaim them ; and their perfeverance in their
oppofition to Chrift and his people, and increafing in all kinds of
wickednefs, while he has been waiting upon them, even to long
fuffering; by inflicting on them fevere and awful judgments, and
remarkably fearful punifhments, to vindicate the honour of his
own name; and avenge his church and people, who have been fo
greatly injured, defpifed and trampled upon ; and that it may be
made known by this, as well as in other ways, that the God of
chriftians, the God and Saviour revealed in the Bible, is the true
God. And this will give great inftruction to thofe who fhall be
left, who will have a heart to perceive and underftand. They will
have before their eyes a leffon, fuited moft effectually to teach them
the exceeding depravity and wickednefs of man ; and how real
and dreadful is the divine difpleafure and anger with finners :
How undone and utterly loft forever, all men are, without a
Redeemer and Sanctifier ; by whom they may be recovered from
the power of fin and fatan, and obtain the forgivenefs of their fins,
and the favour of God : How dependent they are on fovereign
grace for all good, for every thing better than complete deftruction ;
by which alone they are diftinguifhed from thofe who perfevere in
their fins, and perifh. And all this will tend to guard them againft
fin, to promote their repentance and humiliation, and to lead
them

them to more earneft, conftant and united prayer to God for mercy, than was ever exercifed before by men: And to afcribe all the favours they fhall receive, which will then be much more abundant than ever before, to the free, fovereign grace of God; and to give him the praife of all.

In the beginning of this feftion it was fuggefted, that by attending to the events which are to take place, according to fcripture prophecy, before the commencement of the Millennium, farther evidence would come into view, that this will not be much fooner or later, than the beginning of the feventh millenary of the world. This evidence has been now produced. The fixth vial is now running, and probably began to be poured out before the end of the laft century, and will continue to run a confiderable part of the next century; under which the power of antichrift is to be greatly weakened, and the way prepared for his utter overthrow: And at the fame time, the chriftian world, and mankind in general, will be fo far from reforming, that they will grow more and more corrupt in doctrine and practice, and greedily run into all manner of vice and wickednefs, until they are prepared for the battle of that great day, and ripe to be cut down and deftroyed, by a feries of divine judgments, which will be inflicted under the feventh vial, and will iffue in the introduction of the Millennium.

The river Euphrates has been drying up, and the way has been preparing, for near a century paft, for the utter ruin of the Pope and the hierarchy of the church of Rome, and the time of the utter overthrow of antichrift appears to be haftening on. But this is not accompanied with any reformation in that church, or in the Greek church, or in the proteftant churches in general: But very much to the contrary appears. Ignorance, error and delufion, and open vice and wickednefs abound, and are increafing; and infidelity is rapidly fpreading in the chriftian world. The unclean fpirits, like frogs, appear to have gone forth to all the kings' courts, and the great men in Chriftendom; and the greateft corruption and abominable vices are fpread among them, and real chriftianity is neglected, run down and oppofed. And the multitude in general, both learned and unlearned, are going the fame way. Deifm, and a multitude of errors which lead to it, and even to atheifm, are increafing. A fpirit of irreligion, felfifh-nefs, pride and worldlinefs, is exceeding ftrong and prevalent, pro-

ducing all kinds of wickedness, and a ftrong and general oppofition to true religion, and the great truths and doctrines of the gofpel. And the heathen world are no more difpofed to become
chriftians, than they ever were : And the way to their converfion
to chriftianity appears to be more obftructed ; and the few attempts that are made to chriftianize any of them, are generally
unfuccefsful. And Mahometans and Jews hate and oppofe
chriftianity as much as ever they did, if not more, and are finking
farther down in ftupidity, ignorance, infidelity, worldlinefs, and
all kinds of vice.

It is certain, that moft of the evil things now mentioned, have
been found among the body of mankind, in a greater or lefs degree,
in all ages ; and the pious friends of God, and true religion, have
complained of, and lamented them. And it is probable, that the
reprefentation now made, will be confidered by many, only as the
revival of the old complaint, by thofe who are of an illiberal,
gloomy caft of mind, and wholly without foundation, in truth
and fact. But this opinion, though it fhould be generally imbibed, and afferted with great confidence, will not be any evidence
that the reprefentation is not true and juft ; but will rather ferve
to confirm it. For it is commonly, if not always, the cafe, that
in times of great degeneracy, and the prevalence of ignorance,
error and vice, they who are the greateft inftances of it, and moft
funk into darknefs and delufion, are deluded in this alfo, and
entertain a good opinion of themfelves, and of others who join
with them, being ignorant of their true character. They put
darknefs for light, and light for darknefs, and call evil good, and
good evil. And while real chriftianity and true virtue, founded
upon principles of truth and genuine piety, are abandoned, oppofed
and forfaken, they perceive it not, but think all is well, and much
better than before. And they may undertake to *reform chriftianity*,
and think it is greatly reformed, when every doctrine and duty
is excluded from it, which is contrary to the felfifhnefs, pride, and
worldly fpirit of man, and little or nothing is left of it, but the
mere name, to diftinguifh it from the religion of infidels or heathen ; and nothing to render it preferable to thefe.

An appeal muft be made, in this cafe, from the judgment of
thofe of this character, to thofe who are born of the Spirit of God ;
are created in Chrift Jefus unto good works ; by which they are
become new creatures, and turned from the darknefs of this world,

to marvellous light : Who are not conformed to this world, but have overcome it, and are transformed by the renewing of their minds, fo as to know and diftinguifh what is that good and acceptable and perfect will of God, which is revealed in the fcriptures. They who are thus fpiritual, judge of all things refpecting the doctrines and duties of chriftianity, in fome good meafure, according to the truth. To fuch, efpecially thofe of them who have a general knowledge of the ftate of religion in the chriftian world, and of the deluge of ignorance, error and vice with which it is overflowed, it is prefumed, the above defcription will not appear exaggerated, and that there are greater ftrides, and fwifter progrefs made in infidelity, and irreligion, error and falfe religon, in vice and all kinds of wickednefs, than have been ever known before ; and that all thefe are more common, have a wider fpread, and are carried to a higher degree at this time, than in former ages ; and threaten to bear down all truth, and real chriftianity before them : And that the appearance of things, in this refpect, is juft fuch as might be reafonably expected when the unclean fpirits like frogs, the fpirits of devils, are gone forth with a licenfe and defign to fpread their influence among men, and deceive and corrupt the whole world.

There is reafon to conclude, from what has already taken place of this kind, and from the prophecy of thefe unclean fpirits, that they have not yet finifhed their work ; but that the world, efpecially that part of it called chriftian and proteftant, will yet make greater and more rapid advances, in all kinds of moral corruption, and open wickednefs, till it will come to that ftate in which it will be fully ripe, and prepared to be cut down by the fickle of divine juftice and wrath : And it may take near half a century from this time for thefe evil fpirits to complete their work, and gather the world to this battle. But during this time, whether it be longer or fhorter, and before the battle fhall come on, there will probably be great and remaikable judgments, and fore, unufual and furprifing calamities, in one place and another, fuited to awaken and warn mankind, and lead them to fear God, repent and reform ; which being by moft difregarded and abufed, will become the occafion of greater hardnefs of heart and obftinacy, which will be a prelude and provocation to the battle of that great day, in which mankind will be deftroyed in the manner, and to the degree, which has been defcribed above. This battle, as has been before

T 2                                         obferved,

obferved, will not be fought and finifhed at once ; but by a feries of different and increafing calamities and fore punifhments, mankind will be reduced and brought down, and every high thing levelled to the ground, in which the hand of God will be remarkably vifible, and his arm of power and vengeance made bare.— And it may take more than a century to effect all this, in the wifeft and beft manner ; fo that it will not be finifhed till near the beginning of the feventh millenary of the world.

It has been obferved, that while antichrift is coming down, and the way preparing for the utter extinction of the church of Rome, and all her appendages, the world in general, and efpecially the chriftian world, will make fwift advances in delufion and all kinds of wickednefs ; and infidelity will make great progrefs, under the influence of the fpirits of devils, which are gone forth to the whole world. And it may be here obferved, that the increafe and fpreading of this wickednefs, and fpirit of infidelity, will doubtlefs be the means of weakening and preparing the way for the overthrow of that church. The ten horns, or kings, which fhall hate the whore, and make her defolate and naked, and eat her flefh, and burn her with fire, will do this from a felfifh, worldly fpirit, and under the influence of infidelity, and oppofition to all kinds of religion. And the prevalence of deifm and atheifm in popifh countries and nations, which are the natural fruit and offspring of the abominable practices and tyranny of the antichriftian church, has been the means of expofing the fuperftition and wickednefs of that church, and weakening the papal hierarchy. And deifts, and other wicked men, may be made the inftruments of pulling down that antichriftian fabrick yet farther ; as the heathen Romans were of deftroying the corrupt church of Ifrael. If fo, the fall of the Pope will be fo far from implying a revival of true religion ; that it may be attended with the contrary, viz. infidelity, immorality, and all kinds of wickednefs, as the means of it, fo far as it will be effected by the inftrumentality of men.

WHEN John is defcribing the vifion under the fixth vial, of the unclean fpirits like frogs, going forth to the whole world to gather them to the battle, he ftops before he has finifhed the relation, and Jefus Chrift himfelf fpeaks the following words : " Behold, I come as a thief. Bleffed is he that watcheth and keepeth his garments, left he walk naked, and they fee his fhame."\* By which

he

\* Rev. xvi. 15.

he warns thofe in particular, who fhall live when this vial is poured out, of their danger of being feduced by thofe evil fpirits, and
thofe who are corrupted by them, and behaving unworthy of their
chriftian charaĉter ; and fets before them the ftrongeft motives to
deter them from apoftacy, and induce them to be faithful to him,
to *watch and keep their garments* : To continue fpiritually awake,
and properly attentive to all thofe things which concern them as
chriftians ; to their fituation and ftate, their own exercifes and
conduĉt, to the caufe of Chrift, and the enemies with whom they
are furrounded ; to maintain their chriftian profeffion, and aĉt a-
greeable to it, in the exercife of all chriftian graces ; trufting in
the great Captain and General, who only can fave them, and his
church ; and waiting for him with a patient continuance in well
doing. *He comes as a thief.* The thief does not make his prefence and defigns known to any but thofe who are joined with
him, being his friends, and engaged in the fame defign with him.
So, though Chrift be prefent with his church and people, and is in
the midft of his enemies, having all men and devils in his hands ;
and ordering and conducing every thing that is done by them, in
this time of the greateft degeneracy, and high handed wickednefs ;
and knows how to anfwer his own ends by it and them, and to
proteĉt his people, and bring the wheel over his enemies ; yet, in
this his coming and prefence, he is not feen or thought of by the
corrupt, wicked world : They think nothing of his prefence, and
fee not his hand : He is feen only by his friends, who are engaged
in the fame caufe with him, who watch and keep their garments.
They fee his hand in all thofe things, behold him prefent, and
doing his own work ; and are proteĉted from all evil by him,
while the wicked fall into mifchief, and are deftroying themfelves.
And when he comes forth to the battle, and rifes up to the prey, and
to punifh the world for their wickednefs, the wicked will not fee
him, they will not know their danger, or believe he is come, or
will come, till evil falls upon them, and it is too late to efcape.
" For when they fhall fay, Peace and fafety ; then fudden de-
ftruĉtion cometh upon them ; and they fhall not efcape."* And
they only are fafe, who watch and keep their garments, and fee
and adore his hand and prefence, in all his works of terror and
wrath. " Be wife now therefore, O ye kings ; be inftruĉted, ye
judges of the earth. Serve the Lord with fear, and rejoice with
trembling.

* 1 Theff. v. 3.

trembling. Kifs the Son, left he be angry, and ye perifh from the way, when his wrath is kindled but a little. Bleffed are all they that put their truft in Him."*

It is of the greateft importance to chriftians, who live at this day, and thofe who fhall live in the time when the battle fhall come on, that they fhould attend, and difcern the figns of the times, and watch and keep their garments; as this is the only way to be fafe and happy. Our Lord gave the fame direction and command, as to fubftance, when he was on earth, with reference to thefe fame events : " Take heed to yourfelves, left at any time your hearts be overcharged with furfeiting and drunkennefs, and cares of this life, and that day come upon you unawares. For as a fnare fhall it come on all them who dwell on the face of the whole earth. Watch ye therefore, and pray always, that ye may be accounted worthy to efcape all thofe things that fhall come to pafs, and to ftand before the Son of man."†

It will probably be fuggefted, that the reprefentation of fuch a dark fcene, and evil time, to take place before the Millennium will come, is matter of great difcouragement, and tends to damp the fpirits and hopes of chriftians, and to difcourage them from attempting to promote it, or praying for it ; efpecially as it is fet fo far off from our day : So that none in this or the next generation are like to fee it.

To fuch fuggeftions it is eafy to reply,

1. If it be true, and clearly and abundantly foretold, that fuch evils are to take place, before the profperous ftate of the church comes on, it is proper and defirable that all fhould know it, and attend to it, and it cannot be of any difadvantage to any, to know the truth in this cafe, but the contrary. This is revealed to the church for the inftruction and benefit of chriftians, that they may be informed and warned of what is coming, and be prepared for it, and not be difappointed in their expectations, and furprifed when it fhall take place ; but when they fee thefe things coming to pafs, their faith may be ftrengthened, and they lift up their heads and rejoice, knowing that the redemption, the deliverance and profperity of the church draweth near.

2. Thefe evils, both natural and moral, however undefirable and dreadful, in themfelves, are neceffary for the greateft good of

the

* Pfalm ii. 10, 11, 12.     † Luke xxi. 34, 35, 36.

the church of Chrift, and to introduce the Millennium in the beft manner, and there will be then, and forever, more holinefs, joy and happinefs, than if thefe evils had never taken place. In this view, they are kind and merciful difpenfations to the church. The Apoftles and Prophets, and all the inhabitants of heaven, are reprefented as rejoicing in the evils, the punifhment and deftruction of the enemies of Chrift and his church.* The affliction and fervitude of the children of Ifrael in Egypt, and the wickednefs, oppreffion and cruelty exercifed towards them by Pharaoh and the Egyptians ; and the fucceffive calamities and punifhments brought on them by the hand of God, and their final overthrow and deftruction in the Red Sea, were an unfpeakable advantage to the former, and afforded matter of joy and praife. Therefore, chriftians may now not only acquiefce, but even rejoice in thefe events, as ordered by God for wife ends, and neceffary, in order to the greateft difplay of his righteoufnefs and goodnefs, and to promote the beft good and greateft happinefs of his church.

3. God revealed to Abraham the evils which were coming on his pofterity in Egypt, previous to their deliverance and profperity, and the wickednefs and punifhment of the Egyptians ; not to difcourage him, and fink his fpirit, but to fupport and animate him, and ftrengthen his faith; and this did not damp his joy ; but in the view of the whole, he rejoiced. And Jefus Chrift foretold to his difciples the great evils which were coming on them, upon the Jews, the church and the world, not to difcourage and dejeât them, but that they might be forewarned, and expeât them, fo as not to be difappointed when they came, but have their faith confirmed, and poffefs their fouls in patience when the dark fcene fhould come on ; and that they might be encouraged and rejoice, confidering thefe events as tokens that their deliverance was at hand. He therefore faid unto them, " And when thefe things begin to come to pafs, then look up, and lift up your heads ; for your redemption draweth nigh."† This may be applied to chriftians now. While you fee the world gathering to the battle of the great day of God Almighty, and view this battle near at hand, lift up your heads and rejoice, that the church has got fo near the end of darknefs and affliction ; and that the happy day of her deliverance and profperity is fo near at hand.

4. As

---

* Rev. xviii. 20. xix. 1—6.     † Luke xxi. 28.

4. As to the diftance of that happy day of falvation from this time; two hundred years, or near fo many, will pafs off before it will arrive, according to the calculation which has been made from fcripture ; fo that none, now on the ftage of life, will live to fee and enjoy it on earth. But much may be done by chriftians who live in this age, to promote its coming on in the proper time, by prayer, and promoting the intereft of religion, and the converfion of finners : For that good day would not come, unlefs the caufe of Chrift be maintained to that time, and finners be converted to keep up the church, and prevent the total extinction of it. In order to this, thoufands muft be converted, and there muft be a fucceffion of profeffing and real chriftians down to that day. The doctrines, inftitutions, and duties of chriftianity, muft be maintained ; and there will doubtlefs be remarkable revivals of religion in many places, and knowledge will increafe among true chriftians, and there will be advances made in the purity of doctrines and worfhip, and all holy practice, by bringing all thefe nearer to the ftandard of the holy fcriptures : And the churches will be formed into a greater union with each other ; being more and more conformed to the divine pattern, contained in the Bible. Here then is work enough to do, by thofe who defire and are looking for fuch a day, to prepare the way for it, and it may be introduced in the proper time ; and there is no want of encouragement to do it, even in this view, to be ftedfaft and unmoveable, always abounding in the work of the Lord, for as much as they may know, that their labour will not be in vain in the Lord.\*

And chriftians may now have a great degree of enjoyment of that day, and joy in it, though they do not expect to live on earth till it fhall come. True chriftians are difinterefted and benevolent to fuch a degree, that they can enjoy and rejoice in the good of others, even thofe who may live many ages hence, and in the good and profperity of the church, and the advancement of the caufe and kingdom of Chrift in this world, though they fhould not live to fee it. The ftronger their faith is, that this good day is coming, and the clearer and more conftant view they have of it, and the more defirable it appears to them, that there fhould be fuch a time ; the higher enjoyment, and greater joy they will have in it, and in the profpect of it. Thus Abraham looked forward by his faith, and faw this day of Chrift, when all the nations of the earth

\* 1 Cor. xv. 58.

earth fhould be bleffed in him, and derived great comfort and joy in this profpeft. "Your father Abraham rejoiced to fee my day; and he faw it, and was glad."* Chriftians know that it will come on in the beft time, as foon as it can be introduced by infinite wifdom and goodnefs : That there is no delay, but "God will haften it in his time." In this fenfe, Chrift will come *quickly* to fet up his kingdom in the whole world. He is on his way, coming as faft and as foon as he can, confiftent with infinite wifdom. He is preparing the way, and ordering every thing in the beft manner, fo as in the moft proper time, to reign with his church on earth ; and no time is loft. And what chriftian can defire that it fhould be fooner, or before this time ? Is it not enough that Jefus Chrift has undertaken it, and will bring it on in the beft manner, and the fitteft time ? And muft not this give joy to every real chriftian ?

It is farther to be obferved, that though the chriftians who live at this day, will not fee the Millennium come while they are in the body on earth ; yet they will fee and enjoy it, when it fhall come, in a much higher degree than they could do, were they living on earth ; or than thofe who will live on earth at that day. The powers, knowledge and views of the fpirits of the juft made perfeft, are greatly enlarged in heaven, and they have a more clear and comprehenfive view of the works of God, and a more particular knowledge of what is done in this world, efpecially of what relates to the work of redemption, the falvation of finners, and the profperity of the church and caufe of Chrift. There is joy in the prefence of the angels over *one finner* that repenteth. The fpirits of the juft made perfeft are with the angels, and muft know all that paffes in their prefence ; and muft rejoice in fuch an event, as much or more than they. How great muft be their joy then, when whole nations, yea, all the world, become true penitents, and they fee and know this, and what is implied in it, unfpeakably to better advantage, and more clearly, than any can do who fhall be then on earth !

The more chriftians labour and fuffer on earth, in the caufe of Chrift ; and the more they defire, pray for, and promote his coming and kingdom in this world, the more they will enjoy it in heaven, when it fhall take place, and the greater will be their joy

U                                                                    **and**

* John viii. 56

and happinefs. And it will be unfpeakably more and greater in heaven, than if they were in bodies on earth. Who then can reafonably defire to live in this world, merely to fee and enjoy the happy day of the Millennium.

On the whole, it is hoped that it does appear from what has been faid in this differtation, that there will be a thoufand years of profperity of the church of Chrift, in this world; that this is abundantly foretold and held up to view in the Bible; that this will be about the feventh millenary of the world; that it will be a moft happy and glorious day, in which the chriftian difpenfation fhall have its proper and full effect on earth, in the falvation of men; to which all the preceding times and events are preparatory: That the degeneracy and increafing prevalence of ignorance, error and wickednefs now in the world, efpecially in Chriftendom, is preparing for, and haftening on the battle of that great day of God Almighty, in which mankind will be punifhed, and the greateft part then on earth deftroyed; and then the Millennium will be introduced:—That this is an important and pleafing fubject, fuited to fupport and comfort chriftians in all the dark and evil days which precede it, and to excite them to earneft, conftant, united prayer for this coming of Chrift, and patient waiting for him, and to conftant exertions in all proper ways, to promote his intereft and kingdom in the world.

AFTER the thoufand years of the reign of Chrift and his church on earth, "Satan fhall be loofed out of his prifon, and fhall go out to deceive the nations which are in the four quarters of the earth, Gog and Magog, to gather them together to battle: The number of whom is as the fand of the fea. And they went up on the breadth of the earth, and compaffed the camp of the faints about, and the beloved city: And fire came down from God out of heaven, and devoured them."\* In thefe words there is reference to what is faid of Gog and Magog, in the thirty eighth and thirty ninth chapters of Ezekiel: Which prophecy, there is reafon to think, is not to be underftood literally, but in a figurative fenfe; as no events have ever taken place anfwerable to this reprefentation, if taken in a literal fenfe. The prophecy of Gog and Magog,

may

\* Rev. xx. 7, 8, 9.

may be confidered as having reference to two events, which are
to take place at different times, and are fimilar in fome refpects,
and differ in others, viz. The great and general corruption and
wickednefs of mankind, and their punifhment and deftruction
which will precede the Millennium, which has been defcribed in
this fection ; and the apoftacy and wickednefs of mankind at the
end of the Millennium, and the remarkable overthrow and deftruction of them, when Chrift fhall come to judgment ; predicted in
the words which have been now tranfcribed.  Some things faid
of Gog and Magog, of their defigns, doings, and their punifhment, and a number of expreffions in that prophecy, are more
applicable to the former of thefe events than to the latter, and
fome more applicable to the latter than to the former, and the
whole cannot be well applied to one, exclufive of the other ; but
in beth, the prophecy is completely fulfilled.  Both thefe events
refpect wicked men, who have arrived to a great degree of obftinacy and wickednefs; and they are both gathered together by the
agency and deception of fatan, let loofe for that end.  And they
are both gathered together to battle againft Chrift and his church ;
and are deftroyed in the battle.

This prophecy is figurative.  It is not to be fuppofed that all
this great multitude will be gathered together into one place ; or
that the church will be encamped together in one fpot on earth,
or collected in one city : But the gathering of the wicked, means
their being abandoned to infidelity, and a very great degree
of wickednefs, in oppofition to the church of Chrift, and true
religion, and being difpofed to extirpate thefe from the face of
the earth.  In this fenfe, the wicked will be gathered together to
battle, before the Millennium, by the fpirits of devils, or fatan,
who will go forth to the whole world for that end, as has been
explained.  The church will become fmall, and furrounded and
affaulted by the wicked on every fide, and ready to be fwallowed
up, and totally deftroyed by them.

It has been a queftion, from whence this multitude of people,
here called Gog and Magog, fhould come, after the church of
Chrift and true religion had prevailed in the world a thoufand
years ?  Some have fuppofed, that a number of people, and perhaps whole nations, would live in fome corner of the earth, during

the time of the Millennium, without partaking of any of the blessings of it; but will continue in a state of heathenism and wickedness all that time, till at length they will multiply so much, as to be able to rise in opposition to the church, and destroy it, were they not prevented by the miraculous interposition of heaven. And many have supposed, that this fact is inconsistent with all the inhabitants of the world being real christians, and eminently holy in the time of the Millennium. But this supposed difficulty may be easily solved; and the general and great apostacy accounted for, consistent with the supposition, that in the Millennium all mankind will be real christians. Near the end of the thousand years, the divine influences, which produced and continued the universal and eminent holiness in the Millennium, may be in such a measure withheld, as that real christians will, in their exercises and conduct, sink much below what had taken place before, and indulge a careless and worldly spirit to a great and sinful degree, and become more and more negligent of their duty, especially with respect to their children; and be really guilty of breaking covenant with God, in this important point. In consequence of this, their children will not be regenerated and converted; but grow up in a state of sin, real enemies to God and to the truth. And as the world will be then full of people, it will in this way soon become full of wicked men, and the church will be very small. And those who will grow up under the power of sin and satan, in the face of all that light, truth and holiness, which had taken place through the Millennium, and in opposition to it, will naturally arrive to a great and amazing degree of hardness and obstinacy in sin, and become a far more guilty and perverse generation of men, than ever existed before; and will be greater enemies to truth and righteousness, and the church of Christ. And consequently will be united and engaged to banish all these from the earth. The world will have more wicked persons in it than ever before; and all these much more sinful, and engaged in all kinds and ways of opposition to Christ and his cause and people. The church will be on the brink of ruin, just ready to sink and be swallowed up; and the appearance and coming of Christ will be less believed, expected or thought of, than at any other time. Then Christ will be revealed from heaven in flaming fire, taking vengeance on them who know not God, and obey not the gospel.

This

This apoftacy and great wickednefs of fo many millions of mankind, the number of whom will be as the fand of the fea, and their confequent mifery, is an awful difpenfation indeed, and is, in itfelf, an evil infinitely beyond the comprehenfion of man. But there is the cleareft evidence, and the greateft certainty, that this inftance of evil, as well as all other evil which precedes it, and will fucceed it, though it will be endlefs, will, by the overruling hand of God, be productive of overbalancing good ; and is necef- fary, in order to effect the greateft poffible good to the univerfe. " *Surely* the wrath of man fhall praife thee : The remainder of wrath fhalt thou reftrain."* This event will ferve to fet the total depravity, and the ftrong propenfity of man to the greateft degree of wickednefs, in a more clear and ftriking light than it had been, or perhaps could be before. That man fhould apoftatize, and fo foon arrive to fuch a high degree of wickednefs, after all the light and holinefs, and the wonderful goodnefs of God to man, difplayed in the Millennium ; and, in oppofition to all this light and grace, and in the greateft abufe of it, join in rebellion againft God, and trample on his authority, truth and goodnefs, contrary to the ad- monitions and warnings from the word of God, and all faithful minifters and chriftians ; will make a new difcovery, and greater than was ever made before, of fallen human nature, and of the great and defperate evil that is in the heart of man ; and that it is utterly incurable by any means that can poffibly be ufed, fhort of the almighty energy of the Spirit of God, by which the heart is renewed; and confequently of the guilt and infinite ill defert of man ; which difcovery will be of great advantage to the church and kingdom of Chrift forever, and neceffary for the greateft hap- pinefs and glory of it, and the higheft honour of the Redeemer.

And this will make, from fact, a new and greater difcovery of the abfolute dependence of man on the grace and Spirit of God, to prevent his greateft wickednefs and endlefs deftruction, and to form him to holinefs and happinefs ; and of the great and fover- eign grace of God, in converting and faving loft man, and in bringing on fuch a wonderful degree of holinefs and happinefs, and continuing it a thoufand years ; and that this is all to be af- cribed to the fovereign power and grace of God, who has mercy on whom he will have mercy, and whom he will he hardeneth.

When

* Pfalm lxxvi. 10.

When all men fhall be righteous and holy from generation to generation for a thoufand years, and all the children which fhall be born in that time, fhall appear to be pious and holy as foon as they begin to act, and perfevere in this to the end of life, the appearance will be, that mankind are now grown better, and that the evil nature of man is not fo great ; but he is naturally inclined to obedience and holinefs : The fudden and great apoftacy which will take place, will take off this appearance ; and fhow, that the heart of man is naturally as full of evil as ever it was ; and that all the good and holinefs of the Millennium ftate, was the effect of the power of the Spirit of God, and to be wholly afcribed to the infinite, fovereign grace of God. And this difcovery will be remembered by the redeemed forever, and improved to the glory of God, to the praife of rich, fovereign grace, and confequently to their own eternal advantage.

EVEN fo, come LORD JESUS.

AMEN.

*ERRATA.*

Page 14, line 10, for *moon* read *men*
  15,   14 from bot. for *by* r. *of* Chrift
  25,   17, for *foretold* r. *foretell*
  54,   4 from bot. for *virtuous* r. *victorious*

Page 61, line 13, for *moral* read *natural*
  66,   6, for *profefs* r. *poffefs*
  68,   11 from bot. for *profeffing* r. *poffeffing*
  87,   21, dele *not*

*Religion in America*
*Series II*

An Arno Press Collection

Adler, Felix. **Creed and Deed:** A Series of Discourses. New York, 1877.

Alexander, Archibald. **Evidences of the Authenticity, Inspiration, and Canonical Authority of the Holy Scriptures.** Philadelphia, 1836.

Allen, Joseph Henry. **Our Liberal Movement in Theology:** Chiefly as Shown in Recollections of the History of Unitarianism in New England. 3rd edition. Boston, 1892.

American Temperance Society. **Permanent Temperance Documents of the American Temperance Society.** Boston, 1835.

American Tract Society. **The American Tract Society Documents,** 1824-1925. New York, 1972.

Bacon, Leonard. **The Genesis of the New England Churches.** New York, 1874.

Bartlett, S[amuel] C. **Historical Sketches of the Missions of the American Board.** New York, 1972.

Beecher, Lyman. **Lyman Beecher and the Reform of Society:** Four Sermons, 1804-1828. New York, 1972.

[Bishop, Isabella Lucy Bird.] **The Aspects of Religion in the United States of America.** London, 1859.

Bowden, James. **The History of the Society of Friends in America.** London, 1850, 1854. Two volumes in one.

Briggs, Charles Augustus. **Inaugural Address and Defense,** 1891-1893. New York, 1972.

Colwell, Stephen. **The Position of Christianity in the United States,** in Its Relations with Our Political Institutions, and Specially with Reference to Religious Instruction in the Public Schools. Philadelphia, 1854.

Dalcho, Frederick. **An Historical Account of the Protestant Episcopal Church, in South-Carolina,** from the First Settlement of the Province, to the War of the Revolution. Charleston, 1820.

Elliott, Walter. **The Life of Father Hecker.** New York, 1891.

Gibbons, James Cardinal. **A Retrospect of Fifty Years.** Baltimore, 1916. Two volumes in one.

Hammond, L[ily] H[ardy]. **Race and the South:** Two Studies, 1914-1922. New York, 1972.

Hayden, A[mos] S. **Early History of the Disciples in the Western Reserve, Ohio;** With Biographical Sketches of the Principal Agents in their Religious Movement. Cincinnati, 1875.

Hinke, William J., editor. **Life and Letters of the Rev. John Philip Boehm:** Founder of the Reformed Church in Pennsylvania, 1683-1749. Philadelphia, 1916.

Hopkins, Samuel. **A Treatise on the Millennium.** Boston, 1793.

Kallen, Horace M. **Judaism at Bay:** Essays Toward the Adjustment of Judaism to Modernity. New York, 1932.

Kreider, Harry Julius. **Lutheranism in Colonial New York.** New York, 1942.

Loughborough, J. N. **The Great Second Advent Movement:** Its Rise and Progress. Washington, 1905.

M'Clure, David and Elijah Parish. **Memoirs of the Rev. Eleazar Wheelock, D.D.** Newburyport, 1811.

McKinney, Richard I. **Religion in Higher Education Among Negroes.** New Haven, 1945.

Mayhew, Jonathan. **Observations on the Charter and Conduct of the Society for the Propagation of the Gospel in Foreign Parts;** Designed to Shew Their Non-conformity to Each Other. Boston, 1763.

Mott, John R. **The Evangelization of the World in this Generation.** New York, 1900.

Payne, Bishop Daniel A. **Sermons and Addresses,** 1853-1891. New York, 1972.

Phillips, C[harles] H. **The History of the Colored Methodist Episcopal Church in America:** Comprising Its Organization, Subsequent Development, and Present Status. Jackson, Tenn., 1898.

**Reverend Elhanan Winchester:** Biography and Letters. New York, 1972.

Riggs, Stephen R. **Tah-Koo Wah-Kan; Or, the Gospel Among the Dakotas.** Boston, 1869.

Rogers, Elder John. **The Biography of Eld. Barton Warren Stone, Written by Himself:** With Additions and Reflections. Cincinnati, 1847.

Booth-Tucker, Frederick. **The Salvation Army in America:** Selected Reports, 1899-1903. New York, 1972.

Satolli, Francis Archbishop. **Loyalty to Church and State.** Baltimore, 1895.

Schaff, Philip. **Church and State in the United States** or the American Idea of Religious Liberty and its Practical Effects with Official Documents. New York and London, 1888. (Reprinted from *Papers of the American Historical Association,* Vol. II, No. 4.)

Smith, Horace Wemyss. **Life and Correspondence of the Rev. William Smith, D.D.** Philadelphia, 1879, 1880. Two volumes in one.

Spalding, M[artin] J. **Sketches of the Early Catholic Missions of Kentucky;** From Their Commencement in 1787 to the Jubilee of 1826-7. Louisville, 1844.

Steiner, Bernard C., editor. **Rev. Thomas Bray:** His Life and Selected Works Relating to Maryland. Baltimore, 1901. (Reprinted from *Maryland Historical Society Fund Publication,* No. 37.)

**To Win the West:** Missionary Viewpoints, 1814-1815. New York, 1972.

Wayland, Francis and H. L. Wayland. **A Memoir of the Life and Labors of Francis Wayland, D.D., LL.D.** New York, 1867. Two volumes in one.

Willard, Frances E. **Woman and Temperance:** Or, the Work and Workers of the Woman's Christian Temperance Union. Hartford, 1883.